A Record of Interments at the Friends Burial Ground, Baltimore, Maryland (est. 1681)

Researched and Compiled by E. Erick Hoopes
Edited by Christina Hoopes

CLEARFIELD

Copyright © 1995 by Emil E. Hoopes and Christina R. Hoopes
All Rights Reserved.

Printed for
Clearfield Company, Inc. by
Genealogical Publishing Co., Inc.
Baltimore, Maryland
1995

International Standard Book Number: 0-8063-4553-5

Made in the United States of America

Table of Contents

Foreword:
A Short History of the Friends Burial Ground _____ v

Introduction:
*Seeking the Interment Records*_____ ix

Note:
On the Numbering of Gravesites _____ xi

Acknowledgements _____ xii

A Record of Interments at the Friends Burial Ground _____ 1

Foreword
A Short History of the Friends Burial Ground

Much of the early history of the Friends Burial Ground at 2506 Harford Road in Baltimore was evidently gathered by an anonymous Quaker writer from Stony Run Meeting minutes and legal documents. The typewritten and annotated account was obtained from the offices of the Stony Run Meetinghouse on North Charles Street.

Evidently written during a lull in the lively history of Baltimore Quakerism, the history begins: "Most of us of the present day enjoy our serene and perhaps uneventful lives, and think that those who have gone before us led also uneventful lives, but a study of the situation, as far as it can be studied from the meagre and uncertain data that we have, coming from a century ago, we find some strenuous characters among our ancestors in the Church, and that there was a 'good deal of human nature in man' even at that time.." Discretion, however, prevented the unknown writer from including anything more than intriguing hints concerning these forebears of the Society of Friends, Baltimore.

According to this account, the earliest known transaction involving the plot of land that would eventually become the Friends Burial Ground was its sale by "John Ensor, planter, " to Richard Taylor, for a consideration of ten shillings, on Dec. 15th, 1710. For some reason, however, John Ensor did not give Richard Taylor an actual deed for this property, but the memorandum or receipt for the ten shillings was signed by John Ensor and Elizabeth Ensor (her mark), in 1713.

The plot was measured out in the early account: "A Parcel or Tract of Land, called 'Friendship,' being taken out of the larger Tract of Land called "Darley Hall, " beginning at a bounded White Oak, running east twenty perches, thence north eight perches, then west twenty perches -- then with a straight line to the first bounded tree and laid out for one acre of Land. "

In addition to the consideration of ten shillings, the history noted, the property was subject to "the Annual rents due the Lord Proprietor, " who was the Lord Baltimore living at that time. According to the unknown author, some of these annual rents were "very curious" -- for example, three "barley corns" or two "Indian Stone Arrowheads" or similar tokens -- and the old deeds demanded that the same be sent annually to England.

Several sources say that a log meeting house was erected at Friendship in 1713-1714 by Patapsco Weekly Meeting of Friends. A bronze plaque erected on a pedestal at the site states: "On this site was erected Patapsco Friends Meeting house 1713. Removed to Aisquith and Fayette Sts. Balto. town 2 mo 22nd 1781"

Further, an 1862 plat of the burial ground indicates a marker in the southwest corner of the wall that marks the "beginning of Friendship."

In 1729, the year Baltimore Town was established, Richard Taylor's will was written and probated. The item pertaining to Friendship reads: "I give and bequeath unto my son Joseph Taylor a lot of land containing one acre of land bought of John Ensor for to build a Meeting House on it the said land; and the house that is on it I give and bequeath for the use of Friends for a Meeting House and Burying Place for Friends for ever or Quakers so called."

Presumably, Friendship remained the focus of Patapsco Weekly Meeting, which affiliated itself with Gunpowder Monthly Meeting sometime after its 1739 establishment and the construction of Old Gunpowder Meeting House in Sparks, Maryland.

As the Baltimore Quaker community grew, however, Friends found it too inconvenient to attend Meeting in the Old Meeting House near Gunpowder. They decided instead to acquire a lot near the City, for a Meeting House and Burial Ground, but still attend the Monthly Meeting at Gunpowder. Previously, they had been assembling at private houses on First Days. In 1773, a log Meeting House was accordingly erected on the Friendship tract.

Following the construction of the log Meeting House, the anonymous historian notes, "a Burial Ground Committee was appointed to see that no improper person be interred in our Grounds. That would seem to have been the chief duty of the Committee. That Committee was composed of William Brown, Joseph Townsend, William Trimble and Elias Ellicott, all good men and true. They had a Recorder for the meeting then, but the births and deaths were not recorded as they occurred."

In 1781, a more substantial brick meeting house was constructed nearby on Aisquith Street, along with a burial ground. The Monthly Meeting was separated from Gunpowder in 1780.

When Joseph Taylor died in 1788, Friendship again changed hands. His will reads: "I give and bequeath unto my cousins Richard Taylor and Samuel Taylor, sons of Thomas Taylor and Joseph Doughday and my friends John Hopkins and Arthur Lewis for ever all my one acre of land called Friendship where on our meeting house was built for the use of Friends for the publick worship of Almighty God."

In 1790-92, when Maryland Yearly Meeting became Baltimore Yearly Meeting and met in Baltimore, Patapsco Meeting was presumably represented. The meeting itself at that time seems, however, to have been experiencing some internal disorder, as the anonymous historian notes wryly: "The minutes of the Preparative Meeting held in Baltimore previous to this time cannot be found. It is perhaps just as well, for the Administration of Discipline recorded therein, it is believed, would not show all the members to have been 'Children of Light.'"

There is also evidence that Patapsco Meeting wanted to expand the Friendship property, for in 1793, a committee was appointed to petition the Maryland General Assembly to be allowed to buy more land. At that time, no religious denomination could legally hold more than one acre of land. A Committee was therefore appointed to petition the General Assembly on 7th mo. 25 - 1793 to permit the Society to hold a greater quantity of land for its purposes.

The Society's growth was also creating a need for improved record-keeping; on 3rd month 31, 1796, a Special Committee was appointed to collect the items of Deaths and Births, and to hand them to the recorder.

Through all of this, however, the actual ownership of Friendship remained in question. As meeting for worship, meeting for business, and actual burials shifted to Aisquith Street, the Harford Road meeting house was abandoned and burials became sporadic. In 1799, heirs of "the original grantors" tried to reclaim Friendship based on abandonment. Judge Luther Martin ruled in favor of Friends ongoing ownership.

Comments the anonymous writer at the close of the early history: "That distinguished Jurist gave a very guarded opinion, in substance, that as the Society had ceased to hold meetings there, or to make regular interments, it may possibly have lost the equitable right in the property they once had, but if it has been used occasionally as a place of burial and not deserted by Friends, or used by any other persons, the removal of the Meeting House will not injure the right of the Society to the property. This opinion, coming from such an authoritative source, seemed to satisfy both parties to the controversity (sic) and the Friends have since had peaceable possession of the property.

"Perhaps a Lawyer not so distinguished and especially if the fee were ample, would have given a flat opinion but such a distinguished Jurist as the Attorney General, gave a more conservative opinion. "

A later historian -- also anonymous -- continued the history into the following two centuries.

Since John Ensor had not given Richard Taylor an actual deed for the property, the way was open for continued challenges. In 1833, the survivor of the four persons to whom Joseph Taylor willed this property and Meeting House consented to sell the Burial Ground Lot to five friends, namely, Joseph Matthews, Townsend Scott, Joseph Davenport, Philip E. Thomas and John Gillingham. The transaction was made for the sum of two hundred dollars, with the property to be held in trust for the purposes and uses intended by the will of Richard Taylor. '

Meeting growth and doctrinal schisms changed the face of Baltimore Quakerism in the ensuing century. Aisquith Street Meeting gave way to Lombard Street Meeting in 1805, then to Park Avenue Meeting in 1888 (following the 1828 split between the Hicksite and Orthodox Friends) and finally to Stony Run in 1949. Orthodox Friends moved from the McKendrie School to Courtland Street, then to Eutaw Street, and finally, in 1929, to their current site at Homewood Friends Meeting on Charles Street.

Friendship, however, was a constant in the changing scene of Friends in Baltimore. Burial Ground Committee minutes show that Park Avenue Meeting purchased land adjacent to Friendship in 1859 for $1,408.10. Plans were made in 1861 to build a dwelling for the sexton and to enclose the burial grounds with an eight-foot wall. In 1876, the avenues were first graveled, and in 1879, a record book was established for burials dating 1861-1874. In this same year, a mausoleum was removed from Aisquith Street to be installed at Friendship.

In 1890, the tool shed was erected and a fireplace heater installed, with a vent to the second floor. The granite and brass pedestal marking site of the 1713 meeting house was installed in 1897. In 1926, when Baltimore City condemned the Aisquith Street burial ground to make way for a playground, remains and stones from 77 graves were removed to Harford Road.

The sexton's dwelling was renovated several times, most extensively in 1985-1986; with vital structural maintenance and repair being required at several points, most recently in 1994. Likewise, the outbuildings, wall and trees have required ongoing upkeep. Over the years, residential and commercial development gradually surrounded Friendship, and in recent years the city's escalating crime rate has on occasion disturbed the (living) residents' tranquility.

Today, though, as in the Nineteenth Century, the early historian's image of the Burial Ground holds true: "We know that many upheaved mounds are there and many stones, some rough-faced from the fields and unmarked, while others tell a short and simple message, all reminders of those who have lived and moved and had their being, some of them forefathers of the hamlet possibly, and prominent members of our Society at one time, but no one can claim them now. They lived in their day and generation, and we respect and venerate their memories, and keep green the sod that lies over their last resting places, and seem to say to us —

Remember friend, as thou passeth by,
As thou art now, so once was I. "

Introduction
Seeking the Interment Records

The written history of the Friends Burial Ground hints at the difficulties that were involved in the five-year process of assembling a record of interments..

Between the mid-1770's and 1796, burials at Friendship were screened by the Burial Ground Committee. No death records were kept, however, until 3rd month 31, 1796. Even then, the archives preserved information on the members only, rather than on the locations of their graves.

For this reason, there can be no certainty of either the number of burials or the identity of those interred before the mid-Nineteenth Century. Due to Quaker convictions of simplicity, graves from that period are minimally marked; as the anonymous historian wrote, "many upheaved mounds are there and many stones, some rough-faced from the fields and unmarked...no one can claim them now."

The earliest record of burials available at Stony Run Meeting was kept between 1856 and 1898, and lists only the names of those interred. A second book was started in 1889 and cross-referenced with this record.

The archives multiplied and grew more complex as time passed:
- minutes of monthly Burial Ground Committee meetings included names of members buried, but no further information on gravesites
- three books (9b, 10a, and 14a) were created by different Burial Ground Committees for purposes unknown
- a book was created in 1923 to record those who had paid for perpetual care
- a set of index cards was compiled in 1966 to cross-reference burials
- a map was also created in 1966 by Stony Run member Sandy Adams to record the burial ground layout and locations of individual gravesites

By 1988, when sexton Erick Hoopes began to compile a complete and definitive database, even the Stony Run Burial Ground Committee had no idea of the total number of burials, or the location of individual gravesites. Gravedigger Frances Fergusen held some knowledge from longtime sexton John Mason, but even so, the picture was incomplete at best: occasionally new graves would be dug, only to be found already occupied. The best estimate of total interments stood about 1692.

Using the 1966 map, Erick Hoopes consulted the "short and simple message(s)" on the gravestones, now badly eroded from years of pollution. Many had deteriorated so far as to be unreadable. To gather their information, he toured the grounds late at night, using a flashlight to cast sharp light on the inscriptions and reading them by their shadows.

When this phase of the project was completed, with many questions still unanswered, Homewood Meeting member Bob Young lent some assistance. A skilled dowser, he toured the burial ground, disclosing the ages and sexes of those buried in those graves still in question.. A few graves yielded names.. Much of this information was later confirmed through various record books, old burial permits, and meeting correspondence.

Early in the project, it became quite evident that the original, estimated number of interments was badly in error. By the time the project was completed, three years later, the number had risen from 1692 to 1796.

This number, however, and the information contained in this book, are by no means certain. Many names exist on the burial records with no gravesite listed, and many gravesites are known to be occupied, with no name recorded. If the reader has further information, or wishes to correct errors, we gladly welcome comments. Please address correspondence to:

Erick Hoopes
429 Westgate Road
Baltimore, MD 21229

Note
On the Numbering of Gravesites

The Friendship property began as the site of a Meeting House, and did not formally become a burial ground until 1859., when Park Avenue Meeting purchased additional land for this use. At this time, the gravesites were plotted.

The nine sections of the burial ground were identified alphabetically, with their graves identified by section letter and numbered plot (e.g., A1 would identify the first grave in Section A).

In 1926, however, 77 graves were moved from the burial ground of the old Aisquith Street Meeting, and had to be identified according to a different system. They were interred in Section I, which fell within the original boundaries of the Friendship property, and numbered sequentially, starting with 600.

Acknowledgements

We would like to thank the following F/friends and family for their gracious help and encouragement while this record was being compiled:

Mary Dunlap, Stony Run member and archivist, for her invaluable assistance in tracking and discovering the old records

James Dunn, for his knowledge and advice on the mysteries of DBIII

Meghan Hoopes, for her loving patience, her assistance during the midnight research expeditions, and her help in assembling the database

Sandy Reed, for her strong and generous leadership of the Stony Run Burial Ground Committee

Harry Scott, long-time member of the Burial Ground Committee, for his support and historical information

Burial Ground dogs Blackie and Ligeiea, for their good-natured companionship during the long hours of reading the stones

The Friends interred in the Burial Grounds, for their spiritual presence and gentle influence on the project and on our lives.

Finally, to anyone who was involved in the project and is not mentioned above, we offer our thanks.

*A Record of Interments
at the
Friends Burial Ground*

Adams - Arnold

A

Adams Mary Anna (Ann) b. 8/22/1817 d. 12/13/1849 H522 broken stone, end of year date missing
Albaugh Gover Tyson d. 3/24/1910 F89 age 38
Albaugh Henry C. d. 6/3/1886 F90 age 55
Albaugh Sarah Jane d. 4/19/1910 F90 age 71
Albaugh child F91 child of Henry C., F90
Albaugh E. G. C. F92 age 3 m. 11 d., child of Henry C. & Sara J., F90
Albaugh C. E. F92 age 2 d., child of Henry C. & Sara J., F90
Albertson Isaac d. 3/24/1895 E60 age 76, left $1000 legacy to Baltimore Monthly Meeting
Albertson Rebecca T. E64 from 10a book
Albertson John b. 1815 d. 1857 E67 born in New Jersey
Albertson Sarah b. 8/23/1797 d. 9/19/1865 E68
Allnut Thomas d. 1832 I309 listed I308
Allnut Sarah b. 1852 I368
Ambler Mary A.. d. 8/13/1897 age 17 m.., from 1897 minutes
Andrews Mary Elizabeth b. 1869 d. 2/25/1897 E134 age 28
Andrews James B. b. 1836 d. 11/3/1910 E135 age 74, brother of Joseph, J38
Andrews Mary Burgess b. 1838 d. 3/4/1922 E136
Andrews Estelle Taylor d. 4/2/1950 J36 age 82
Andrews Estelle F. J37 from 3x5 card, possibly Estelle T., J36
Andrews Anna Burgess b. 4/3/1843 d. 7/29/1936 J37
Andrews Joseph W. b. 5/28/1838 d. 12/7/1915 J38 brother of James
Anthony Ellen A. b. 9/27/1830 d. 9/17/1914 A163
Applegarth Albert C. b. 2/25/1864 d. 3/20/1918 E18 husband of Mary P., E186
Applegarth Mary Penrose b. 11/22/1869 d. 6/2/1958 E186 wife of Albert C., E185
Arnold child of C.M. d. 4/22/1897 from 1897 minutes and 9B

1

Atkinson - Balderston

Atkinson Mary Jane Lewis d. 9/13/1891 I25 age 80, no stone
Atkinson Maria I26 no stone, possibly also James Atkinson
Atkinson Israel I29 no stone
Atkinson M.H. I30 no stone, possibly Mahlon
Ayres Dorothy Corse b. 3/14/1896 d. 12/17/1918 C53 was nurse at Hopkins

B

B. D. d. 1825 661
B. J. B. (A.) I369
Bagby Anne Campbell b. 6/4/1899 d. 5/2/1978 A264
Bagby Janet Campbell b. 1/9/1870 d. 10/16/1951 A265 last name Ritchie on permit
Bagby Alfred Jr. b. 9/18/1866 d. 7/6/1948 A266
Baker Dr. Herbert H. d. 10/10/1928 A187 no stone
Baker Elizabeth McPherson d. 6/4/1940 A187 age 59 y. 6 m. 14 d., no stone
Baker Theodore Emmons b. 8/20/1907 d. 3/7/1993 J42 son of Conrad E. Baker & Alice I. Emmas; husband of Anna W. H., J43
Baker Anna Walton Hull b. 11/10/1907 d. 7/17/1978 J43 no stone, daughter of Thomas B. Hull Jr. & Helen P. Lamb, J44/J45, wife of Theodore, J42
Balderston Margaret b. 6/23/1836 d. 7/17/1887 E165
Balderston Jacob d. 8/25/1881 E166 age 71
Balderston Ruth A. d. 12/12/1874 E167 age 61
Balderston T. H220 fieldstone
Balderston E. Y. H221 fieldstone
Balderston Isaiah d. 1877 H223 age 65
Balderston Martha d. 1817 H224 age 79
Balderston Esther b. 1775 d. 1829 H227
Balderston Eli b. 5/?/1776 d. 4/?/1853 H228
Balderston Mary b. 1814 d. 1833 H229

Balderston Hannah d. 1861 H230 age 43
Balderston Mary C. d. 7/4/1872 H405 age 65
Balderston Wilson d. 5/11/1872 H406 age 68
Balderston Margaret d. 7/17/1870 H407 age 52
Balderston Hugh B. d. 6/14/1860 H408 age 78
Baldwin Dr. John C. b. 3/21/1887 d. 7/3/1939 I399 on map as I400, on permit as H398
Baldwin Ada Case b. 2/3/1887 d. 10/2/1970 I400 on map as I399
Ball Susan F. d. 1844 647
Barker Priscilla b. 12/4/1781 d. 3/29/1817 H219
Barlow infant of Byron A. d. 6/20/1901
Barnes Ruth Anna b. 11/24/1844 d. 4/4/1926 A143
Barnes William J. b. 9/18/1840 d. 11/11/1896 A144
Bartholomeu A. d. 1846 I194
Bartlett Howard M. b. 7/4/1869 d. 11/24/1937 A182
Bartlett Helen C. b. 10/21/1866 d. 7/28/1945 A183
Bartlett Virginia Cowgill b. 5/19/1835 d. 11/7/1920 A184 wife of John K., A185
Bartlett John Kemp Sr. b. 5/5/1832 d. 7/15/1899 A185 husband of Virginia C., A184, in 10a book as A248
Bartlett Elizabeth Hallowell b. 2/24/1890 d. 9/4/1973 A204 daughter of William K. & Juliet R., A205/206
Bartlett Juliet Reese b. 3/27/1855 d. 6/9/1922 A205 wife of William K., A206, daughter of Edward & Mary A. Reese (nee Gilpin), B61/B62
Bartlett William K. b. 11/17/1855 d. 1/9/1930 A206 husband of Juliet R., A205
Bartlett infant (Edith) d. 1886 A206½
Bartlett Edith Kemp d. 1886 A207 age 3 w., daughter of William K. & Juliet R., A205/206
Bartlett Sally (Sallie) Ann d. 9/29/1855 H 98 age 34?
Bartlett Rebecca d. 6/18/1862 H409
Bartlett Mary J. d. 6/19/1852 H410 age 15 m.
Bartlett William A. d. 12/3/1864 H411 age 32?
Bartlett Richard H412

Baynes - Blackburn

Baynes Mary Burrough   b. 7/6/1846   d. 10/31/1876   E52   wife of George B., E53, daughter of Jacob & Elizabeth Burrough, B33/B34
Baynes George B.   b. 11/23/1834   d. 1/30/1891   E53   husband of Mary B., E52
Baynes James P.   b. 7/26/1813   d. 5/12/1885   E83
Baynes John B.   b. 8/25/1833   d. 11/29/1872   E84
Baynes Martha   b. 7/6/1803   d. 10/21/1870   E85
Baynes James   d. 12/25/1872   E 86   age 67, from England 1819
Baynes John   d. 5/31/1857   H57   age 72
Baynes Sarah   d. 7/5/1872   H58   age 64, wife of Joseph P., H59
Baynes Joseph P.   b. 6/25/1809   d. 9/18/1892   H59   husband of Sarah, H58, born in England
Baynes Matilda A.   b. 12/23/1834   d. 11/9/1907   H60
Baynes John B.   H456   fieldstone
Baynes Sarah W.   d. 10/31/1862   H464   age 54
Baynes Thomas   d. 3/25/1877   H465   age 74
Beetlestone   Maude Rose   b. 9/5/1897   d. 4/22/1964   A235
Beetlestone   Guy Clarke   b. 9/4/1898   d. 10/25/1941   A236
Bell   Thomazin Y.   b. 7/8/1809   d. 5/18/1871   H92
Bell   Elizabeth T.   b. 12/10/1791   d. 1/31/1859   H93
Bell   Mary Ann   b. 10/21/1798   d. 7/30/1858   H94
Betterton   R.   d. 1832   E225
Betterton   R. M.   d. 1832   E227
Betterton   G.   d. 1835   E228
Betterton   O. K.   b. 1/13/1822   d. 8/1/1842   E229
Betterton   William Gardner   b. 12/3/1821   d. 8/15/1886   E230
Biddison   Elizabeth M.   b. 1868   d. 1905   J3   wife removed from family burial ground
Birdsall   Ann Maria   d. 1/15/1888   in 9B book
Bishop   Mary M.   b. 10/30/1820   d. 12/5/1891   H149   daughter of Jim & Anna
Blackburn   C. Watson   b. 3/11/1855   d. 9/22/1886   H391   husband of S. Olivia, H392

Blackburn - Broomwell

Blackburn   S. Olivia Coale   b. 8/2/1855   d. 6/26/1889   H392   wife of C. Watson, H391

Blackburn   Cyrus   b. 9/15/1826   d. 8/4/1887   H393   husband of Mary C., H394

Blackburn   Mary C.   b. 11/23/1828   d. 9/5/1917   H394   wife of Cyrus, H393

Blackburn   Maria P.   b. 3/18/1826   d. 11/8/1903   H395   from Chatham, New York, wife of Edwin P., H396

Blackburn   Edwin P.   b. 10/7/1834   d. 11/18/1903   H396   born Bedford County, Pennsylvania, died Denver, Colorado, husband of Maria P., H359

Blackburn   Charles P.   b. 12/8/1858   d. 7/28/1938   H440

Blackburn   Deborah Ferris   b. 4/27/1863   d. 12/17/1947   H441

Blackburn   Mary Ferris   b. 1/17/1890   d. 8/12/1973   H442

Blackburn   Edith Sharpless   b. 7/25/1891   d. 4/15/1988   H443

Blackwell   William C.   d. 11/5/1886   G58   no stone

Blakey   James W.   d. 3/25/1894   G38   age 54, no stone from permit; from 10a book Joseph

Bonsall   Edward   d. 5/31/?   G53   age 59

Bowen   Catherine   b. 3/6/1799   d. 6/7/1883   H298

Bowen   David H.   H304   age 45

Bowen   Elizabeth   H305   age 87

Bowen   infant   H306   no stone

Boyd   Mary   d. 1854   I224

Boyd   Joseph   d. 1847   I281

Bregel   Edith Emily Hartley   b. 3/31/1904   d. 12/29/1971   C181/2   appears to be in C17 in P.C. book, Howard C. has 18, 181/2, 19

Brevitt   Catharine (K.) MacKenzie   b. 5/17/1850   d. 12/6/1945   E72   wife of Edwin Woodland, daughter of Thomas & Elenora I. Mackenzie, E79/E80

Brodbeck   Eliza J.   b. 7/7/1853   d. 2/8/1948   G66

Bromwell   Esther   b. 5/5/1868   d. 10/28/1936   J53   in P.C. book as Broomell

Bromwell   Bertha L.   b. 12/12/1873   d. 5/7/1951   J53

Bromwell   Rebecca J.   b. 9/22/1848   d. 3/20/1924   J54

Broomwell - Brown

Bromwell   Seneca P.   b. 12/24/1840   d. 7/21/1926   J55   in P. C. book as Broomell
Brooks   Alice K.   B53   no stone
Brooks   Samuel M.   d. 4/8/1895   B54   age 76, no stone
Brooks   Laura Virginia   d. 10/28/1909   B55   age 68, no stone
Brooks   Edwin (Edward) M.   d. 9/6/1913   B57   age 35, no stone
Brooks   John G.   d. 11/10/1874   H48   age 3, may have been removed
Brooks   Anna M.   d. 3/3/1938   H141   age 78, no stone
Brooks   C. W.   b. 8/19/1880   d. 8/29/1888   H142
Brooks   William J.   b. 9/1/1826   d. 10/23/1876   H143   husband of Anna M., H144
Brooks   Anna Marie   d. 9/19/1905   H144   wife of William J., H143
Brooks   Sophia   d. 9/14/1882   H145   2nd daughter of William J. & Anna M., H143/144
Brooks   Mary S.   b. /13/1832   d. 11/28/1892   H153
Brooks   William Sr.   d. 8/21/1855   H154   age 84
Brooks   Sophia   d. 9/12/1872   H155   age 83
Brown   Kirk   b. 1845   d. 1/31/1921   C13   age 76
Brown   Mary Florence   b. 1873   d. 1874   C14
Brown   Martha Leila   b. 1848   d. 6/14/1921   C15
Brown   Charles Clemson   b. 1876   d. 2/1/1946   C16   age 69 y. 9 m.
Brown   Henrietta P.   d. 8/13/1833   E236   age 7
Brown   Harriet A.   d. 8/20/1833   E237   age 12
Brown   Charles E.   d. 5/9/1884   F15   age 51
Brown   Sophia H.   d. 11/19/1907   F16   age 80
Brown   Mary M.   d. 11/9/1865   F17   age 62
Brown   George   d. 8/?/1849   G17
Brown   Dorothy   d. 1837   G81
Brown   Jesse   d. 1802   G82
Brown   Ann B.   d. 8/8/1863   H123   age 71
Brown   David   d. 7/31/1838   H124   age 55
Brown   Mary D.   d. 8/28/1867   H125   age 53
Brown   William T.   b. 5/23/1817   d. 8/8/1894   H222
Brown   Diana   d. 1866   H336   age 2 y., #14 book

Brown - Campbell

Brown Uria d. 7/18/1837 H338
Brown Mary d. 3/12/1858 H339
Brown David D (W.) d. 7/3/1853 H340
Brown Ann M. b. 12/2/1811 d. 7/20/1890 H361
Brown John b. 12/30/1801 d. 5/4/1879 H362
Brown Catherine d. 1860 H363 age 80
Brown Catherine H364 age 34
Brown James H364 age 26
Brown John d. 1802 H365 age 54
Brown Mary d. 1855 H365 age 85
Brown Florence M. d. 6/6/1864 H501 age 3
Brown John B. d. 11/26/1852 I102 age 75
Brynan Mary d. 1855 I103
Bullock Martha H. b. 11/22/1832 d. 2/23/1843 680
Burgess Anna E. E130 age 2 m.
Burgess Elizabeth Smith b. 1807 d. 1876 E131
Burgess Amos b. 1801 d. 1886 E132
Burgess William S. b. 1831 d. 11/1/1893 E133 age 63
Burnes H335 no stone
Burrough Jacob b. 5/15/1813 d. 1/6/1881 B33
Burrough Elizabeth b. 11/5/1815 d. 11/16/1904 B34
Burrough Annie G. b. 5/24/1849 d. 7/26/1921 B35
Burrough Samuel Griscom b. 10/6/1833 d. 8/2/1900 B36
Butler John M. b. 1793 d. 1841 I480
Byers child G21 child of Rudolph, no stone

C

Callander Sadie M. J. b. 1885 d. 1976 I88
Campbell John J. d. 6/11/1907 G36 not on stone, see C. Fuhrman
Campbell Anna E. d. 1900 G37 not on stone, see Mary G. Taylor

7

Campbell - Chandlee

Campbell Ella H. d. 8/4/1906 G37 age 25, not on stone; see Mary Taylor
Campbell I230 no stone
Canby Maria L. b. 7/7/1824 d. 11/21/1890 E29 from 1931 book and permit E27
Canby Edwin K. d. 8/8/1880 E28 age 27
Canby Samuel b. 1/4/1808 d. 8/21/1878 E30
Canby William T. b. 4/13/1849 d. 3/28/1886 E31
Canby Julianna Maria d. 7/15/1852 I155 listed in 1931 book as Knight
Canby George B. d. 4/?/1840 I327 age 22 m. 18 d., actual placement at approx. I332, on 3x5 card as I337
Cann Mollie (Mary) S. b. 9/14/1846 d. 10/1/1913 I300
Canty Rachel Hopkins d. 6/5/1928 F131 age 36
Carcaud Elizabeth A. d. 2/7/1922 E211 age 84, no stone
Carcaud Elizabeth G. d. 5/16/1870 E223 age 5 y. 3 m.
Carcaud Charles d. 8/21/1872 E242 age 3 y. 1 m.
Carcaud Thomas b. 2/8/1827 d. 12/24/1901 E243
Carcaud Elizabeth b. 9/27/1836 d. 2/8/1922 E244
Carroll Diana d. 1835 648 age 50
Carroll Pricilla A. d. 1830 G76
Carter Robert Randolph b. 10/28/1912 d. 4/27/1957 A177
Carter George Corse b. 9/3/1906 d. 6/29/1945 A178
Carter Allan Leroy Jr. b 6/4/1904 d. 6/3/1949 A179
Carter Caroline Corse b. 6/4/1871 d. 1/5/1958 A180
Carter Allan Leroy b. 1/26/1871 d. 11/25/1944 A181
Cecil Elizabeth J. b. 1876 d. 11/8/1931 A228 age 55
Cecil Smith b. 1876 d. 6/8/1940 A229 age 63 y. 9 m.
Chandlee Benjamin d. 1834 678
Chandlee Henry, M.D. b. 12/4/1853 d. 4/19/1916 C39
Chandlee Ellis b. 1859 d. 9/26/1942 C39 age 83
Chandlee Anna B. b. 11/6/1854 d. 9/13/1897 C40
Chandlee Franklin F69 from 10a book
Chandlee Edwin d. 11/27/1866 H96 age 16 y. 6 m.
Chandlee Cassandra d. 3/2/1868 H97 age 36

Chandlee - Coburn

Chandlee   Elizabeth M.   d. 4/27/1835   H213   age 77
Chandlee   Benjamin   d. 4/22/1822   H214   age 42
Chandlee   William   d. 1840   I325   age 60, unsure of date
Chapman   E. B.   d. 1843   H274
Chase   Mary Roberts Barnes   b. 11/2/1866   d. 4/27/1967   A141
Chase   Emmett C.   b. 8/31/1858   d. 5/11/1922   A142
Chelfant   Clara Painter   b. 11/29/1836   d. 2/17/1923   E160   Chalfont?
Clapp   Rebecca C.   d. 9/30/1837   H291   age 22
Clark   Drucilla Arabella Lutz   b. 1/21/1905   d. 2/27/1988   A66
Clark   Henry C.   H117   possibly Clarke
Clark   Ann   d. 12/21/1852   H204   age 90
Clark   Benjamin   d. 3/11/1837   I261   10 m.
Clement   Mary Regester Davis   b. 10/31/1862   d. 9/19/1943   F101
Clifford   Harriett Ann   b. 8/19/1819   d. 2/7/1897   C108
Clifford   John   I27   no stone
Clifford   Ellie   I28   no stone
Cloos   Ernst   b. 5/17/1898   d. 5/28/1974   A244
Clow   Grace Thomas   d. 2/28/1976   H36   with Richard H Jr.
Coale   Louise Bartlett   b. 8/22/1882   d. 12/16/1957   A200   wife of Skipwith P., A201
Coale   Skipwith Peyton   b. 11/24/1875   d. 5/30/1922   A201   husband of Louise B., A200
Coale   Amelia   d. 9/15/1859   H74   age 72
Coates   H.   640
Coates   J.   640
Cobb   H497   fieldstone
Cobb   Ruth Alma   d. 5/22/1866   H498   died in Boston, Massachusetts
Cobb   Daniel   d. 10/7/1837   H498   age 45? died in Baltimore County, Maryland
Cobb   Elizabeth   d. 8/14/1897   H499   age 73, died in Providence, Rhode Island
Coburn   Henry   G29   no stone
Coburn   Henry   b. 1816   d. 1874   H523
Coburn   Elizabeth F.   b. 7/30/1836   d. 2/1/1881   H524

Cock - Cornell

Cock Virginia S. b. 6/24/1854 d. 9/14/1855 I47
Cockburn Cyrus B. d. 8/2/1887 permit
Codet Joseph G. (R.) d. 2/13/1904 H429 age 88
Collins Elizabeth W. d. 2/5/1930 C117 age 74, wife of Arthur T. Collins
Collins Arthur W. b. 1890 d. 12/22/1965 C117 age 74, son of Arthur T. & Elizabeth W.
Comegys Elizabeth d. 1849 H242 age 68
Comegys William d. 1830 H243
Comegys D. I121 no stone
Comegys M. I122 no stone
Comegys J. I125 no stone
Conway Arthur d. 1862 I56
Cook Walter d. 1851 I60
Cooksey Helen Waddington b. 5/28/1885 d. 10/24/1923 A135
Corkran Edward T. d. 4/19/1896 F122 age 2½ w., grandchild of R. Virginia, F141, from 1896 minutes
Corkran R. Virginia b. 8/20/1861 d. 11/1/1895 F141 wife of Francis S., F142
Corkran Francis S. Jr. b. 7/15/1856 d. 10/27/1889 F142 husband of R. Virginia, F141
Corkran Mary Louisa d. 6/5/1913 F143 age 81, no stone
Corkran Francis S. d. 11/13/1886 F144 age 7 y. 1 d.
Corkran Mary Elizabeth b. 10/2/1838 d. 3/1/1920 I44 in Lamb plot
Corkran Sarah B. d. 10/24/1852 I74 age 37, buried with Richard Plummer
Corkran child I74 buried with Sarah B.
Corkran Edward S. d. 7/22/1866 I75 age 3, son of Francis S. & Mary Louisa, F143/F144
Cornell Elizabeth H. b. 10/15/1837 d. 12/18/1908 H62
Cornell John J. b. 9/20/1826 d. 2/5/1909 H63
Cornell Harry James b. 7/13/1865 d. 11/1/1904 H489
Cornell Mark J. d. 10/20/1875 H490 age 42
Cornell Francis J. b. 11/11/1834 d. 4/23/1907 H491

Cornell William G. (Y.)   d. 3/4/1864   H492   age 65?
Cornell Theodore   d. 1/15/1864   H493   age 34
Cornthwaite John   d. 1837   626   age 60
Cornthwaite E.   d. 1836   627   age 48
Cornthwaite David W.   b. 8/10/1817   d. 6/19/1878   G15
Cornthwaite John O.   b. 2/22/1809   d. 12/20/1871   G16
Cornthwaite Rachel M.   G16   not on stone
Cornthwaite William P.   d. 12/16/1873   H193   age 56?
Cornthwaite Robert   d. 9/17/1861   H196   age 84
Cornthwaite Alice Ann   d. 1/25/1870   H197   age 81
Cornthwaite Grace Read   d. 1902   I187   no stone
Cornthwaite Matilda Norris   b. 3/21/1866   d. 9/28/1935   I200   (I201) Tillie on stone
Cornthwaite Robert B.   b. 2/20/1864   d. 10/25/1936   I201   (I202)
Cornthwaite Howard C.   b. 5/18/1926   d. 11/13/1928   I202   (I200) son of Elmer B., grandson of Robert C.
Cornthwaite Anita Elizabeth   b. 9/10/1896   d. 8/11/1967   I210   listed on burial permit as I209, maiden name Whiteford
Cornthwaite Arthur R.   b. 6/30/1904   d. 2/16/1936   I211   (I210)
Cornthwaite Henrietta O.   b. 8/12/1899   d. 2/10/1976   I213
Cornthwaite Elmer Burnett   b. 1/15/1892   d. 9/22/1958   I213
Cornthwaite Sarah Long   b. 9/14/1924   d. 5/7/1967   I216
Cornthwaite David Lloyd, M.D.   b. 5/1/1921   d. 11/28/1978   I217
Corse James   d. 6/17/1887   B??   age 76, from permit
Corse William J. C.   b. 7/17/1845   d. 12/21/1932   B132
Corse Ida A.   b. 5/11/1850   d. 6/19/1908   B133
Corse Caroline D.   b. 11/23/1835   d. 11/11/1899   B134
Corse Deborah Sinclair   b. 2/19/1810   d. 7/7/1899   B135
Corse Harry C.   d. 11/16/1899   B135?   child of Deborah, B135, removed from Baltimore cemetery on this date, from 1899 minutes
Corse William   d. 1869   B136   unreadable stone
Corse William Gilbreath   b. 8/18/1895   d. 7/12/1896   C1
Corse Robert Norris   b. 8/18/1895   d. 9/28/1953   C1a
Corse Mary N.   b. 1/11/1871   d. 10/1/1877   C2

Corse - Cowman

Corse   Eunice C.   b. 11/24/1881   d. 7/14/1913   C3   wife of Robert S., C5?
Corse   Rachel S.   b. 2/3/1844   d. 12/6/1923   C4
Corse   Robert Sinclair   b. 5/21/1818   d. 8/22/1917   C5   husband of Eunice C., C3?, appears to be C6
Corse   Dr. George Fox   b. 12/8/1839   d. 3/23/1905   C10
Corse   Sarah Sutton   b. 12/20/1842   d. 3/22/1922   C11
Cowman   Annie   b. 11/5/1866   d. 4/17/1949   B78
Cowman   Arthur   b. 5/21/1861   d. 2/6/1940   B79
Cowman   Sarah   b. 2/22/1822   d 10/6/1909   B80
Cowman   Edward   b. 1/22/1817   d. 12/6/1894   B81
Cowman   Elizabeth   d. 2/1/1952   B82   age 95½, no stone
Cowman   Francis, Robert, Edward   B84   sons of Edward & Sarah, B80/81
Cowman   Caroline Winder   d. 3/17/1938   B108   age 70, no stone
Cowman   James   d. 11/24/1928   B109   age 76, no stone
Cowman   Samuel S.   d. 1891   B117   husband of Anna, B118
Cowman   Anna   b. 6/10/1801   d. 6/11/1887   B118   wife of Samuel S., B117
Cowman   William T.   b. 1840   d. 10/29/1897   B119   age 57
Cowman   Mary   b. 11/2/1885   d. 12/7/1905   B120   daughter of Samuel S. & Anna, B117/B118
Cowman   Martha   b. 10/21/1823   d. 5/10/1911   B121
Cowman   Emily   b. 3/15/1833   d. 2/18/1918   B122
Cowman   Anna Marston   b. 8/29/1834   d. 10/3/1922   B123
Cowman   Helen May   b. 2/9/18?7   d. 7/15/1885   B145   cannot read birth year
Cowman   Herbert F.   b. 5/18/1854   d. 10/15/1855   B146
Cowman   Ellen   b. 1810   d. 1889   B150   wife of Joseph, B151
Cowman   Joseph   b. 5/22/1801   d. 2/18/1872   B151   husband of Ellen, B150
Cowman   Sarah   b. 5/28/1789   d. 7/25/1874   B152
Cowman   Hattie N.   b. 11/16/1839   d. 12/6/1876   B153
Cowman   Ellen   b. 8/26/1841   d. 3/30/1914   B154
Cowman   Annie Rebecca   b. 2/22/1838   d. 3/7/1919   B155
Cowman   Florrie (Flora)   b. 12/31/1875   d. 6/12/1876   B156   child of Lizzie & Charles, B158/B159

Cowman - Dallam

Cowman   Harry   b. 7/2/1881   d. 7/18/1881   B156   child of Lizzie & Charles, B158/B159
Cowman   Robert G.   b. 10/23/1874   d. 8/13/1875   B157
Cowman   Elizabeth (Lizzie) W.   b. 6/28/1818   d. 7/24/1881   B158
Cowman   Rachel C.   B158
Cowman   Charles   b. 9/11/1840   d. 8/2/1921   B159
Cowman   Harriet H.   b. 1/3/1837   d. 4/23/1927   F126
Cowman   Samuel S.   b. 7/28/1836   d. 8/22/1884   F127
Cowman   Harriett H.   d. 12/5/1954   F128   age 85
Cowman   Mattie   d. 12/25/1877   F129   age 14 y. 7 m.
Cowman   Ella   d. 7/23/1940   F130   age 79
Cox   John R.   b. 10/10/1817   d. 11/26/1890   E174   on map as E175
Cox   Joseph H.   b. 3/20/1815   d. 6/8/1868   E175   on map as E174
Cox   Mary Lamb   b. 1/28/1838   d. 5/28/1926   E176   sister of Eli M. Lamb, I40
Cox   John Roberts Jr.   b. 12/8/1875   d. 5/9/1899   E177
Cox   Esther Lamb   b. 8/3/1872   d. 8/25/1974   E178   daughter of John R. & Mary L., E174/E175
Cox   Mary Clara   d. 7/27/1887   F93   age 110
Cox   M.   G93   no stone
Cox   Susan   I23   no stone
Crawford   Thekla   b. 11/6/1872   d. 8/9/1899   I417   daughter of Charles & Catherine
Culbreth   Mary Ann   602   age 29
Culbreth   Ella   b. 9/24/1850   d. 2/3/1924   A164
Culbreth   Elmira   b. 12/23/1815   d. 3/31/1898   A165

D

D.   E. S.   622
Dallam   Eliza   H254
Dallam   Sarah   d. 1833   H255

Dallam - Davis

Dallam William d. 1834 H256
Dallam H. H258
Daran Elizabeth R. b. 6/15/1861 d. 6/30/1938 E681/2
Dare Mary B. d. 4/26/1955 I242 age 89, no stone
Dare Frank M. b. 1856 d. 10/5/1937 I243 age 81
Dare Virginia b. 1866 d. 11/9/1939 I244 age 74
Dare Caroline S. b 12/10/1830 d. 3/4/1914 I245
Dare William H. d 2/10/1891 I246 age 63
Dare Rachel d. 1878 I247
Dare Willie I248
Dare Gideon G. d. 5/19/1899 I254
Dare Catherine McKewen b. 3/26/1890 d. I302 age 68
Dare Catherine d. 9/24/1862 I304 age 73
Dare Lydia M. b. 12/28/1800 d. 12/10/1854 I305
Dare Sarah d. 1833 I306
Dare Margaret P. d. 1832 I315
Dare James G. b. 4/19/1846 d. 1/25/1873 I316
Dare Eliza Jane d. 9/09/1892 I317 age 64
Dare George H. b. 10/3/1839 d. 2/4/1877 I318
Dashield (ell) Emma d. 12/18/1892 G24 age 43, no stone
Dashield (ell) Mary E. d 1/21/1908 G25 age 86, no stone
Davenport C. F. d. 1831 641
Davenport Mary B. H307 age 67
Davenport Joseph H308 age 77
Davenport Jane H. d. 2/10/1879 H309 age 67
Davis Howard Barnard b. 1/2/1890 d. 7/3/1890 C72
Davis Frank d. 1/5/1884 C73
Davis Ernst L. b. 2/26/1885 d. 10/6/1918 C74 husband of Alice Healey Davis
Davis Helen Louise b. 9/5/1888 d. 4/4/1962 C75 daughter of Howard & Ida, C76/C77
Davis Howard b. 8/25/1858 d. 1/14/1924 C 76
Davis Ida Weldon b. 2/19/1858 d. 8/4/1938 C77
Davis Mary d. 2/14/1863 E200 age 1 y. 3 m.

14

Davis - Dawson

Davis Willie   d. 9/16/1870   E201   age 2 m.
Davis Arthur   d. 12/?/1878   E202   age 8 y. 2 m.
Davis George   d. 7/?/1880   E203
Davis Annie   b. 1/8/1866   d. 1/21/1955   E208   daughter of Maria K. & Franklin, E209/E210, born Staunton, Virginia
Davis Maria Kent   d. 3/12/1920   E209   age 86
Davis Franklin   d. 10/15/1895   E210   age 67
Davis Muriel Janney Johns   b. 1/24/1885   d. 1/7/1970   F99   wife of Franklyn D., F100
Davis Franklyn David   b. 3/21/1885   d. 2/15/1945   F100   husband of Muriel J.J., F99
Davis Edwin   b. 12/25/1859   d. 2/3/1898   F102
Davis Thomas R.   F104   unsure of name, possibly Matthews
Davis Georgeanna F. Swann   b. 4/23/1842   d. 1/23/1889   G63 or G65   wife of William F. Swann
Davis Amos   d. 3/15/1842   I269   husband of Elizabeth, I270
Davis Elizabeth   d. 12/11/1849   I270   wife of Amos, I269
Davis Elizabeth C.   d. 2/13/1844   I271   age 16
Davis Ann   d. 12/?/1868   I272   age 56
Dawson Isaac   G52   unreadable stone
Dawson Edith Mathews   b. 10/13/1858   d. 8/1/1911   H84   daughter of William P. & Mary J., H85/86
Dawson William Powell   b. 5/11/1828   d. 2/16/1905   H85   husband of Mary J., H86
Dawson Mary J.   b. 9/19/1832   d. 6/12/1893   H86   wife of William P., H85
Dawson Harriet D.   d. 1859   H146   age 23
Dawson William D. Jr.   d. 1870   H147   age 71
Dawson Harriet T.   b. 2/14/1810   d. 2/17/1885   H148
Dawson Thomas M.   b. 9/21/1864   d. 6/30/1945   H159   son of W.P. & Mary J., H85/H86
Dawson Minnie Mora   b. 4/18/1878   d. 7/4/1963   H159   not on stone, buried with Thomas M. her husband
Dawson Ann   H160   age 85
Dawson William D.   d. 1852   H161

DeBruyn - Dunham.

DeBruyn   Adrianne   b. 3/18/1876   d. 9/26/1881   G44
Denk   Eugene H.   b. 10/30/1916   d. 5/6/1958   A278   wife Ruth, teacher Friends School
Denton   Emma Gillingham Wilson   d. 11/9/1914   E55   age 49, wife of Joseph S.
Dickerson   d. 1856   653   age 31 y. 21 d.
Dickerson   Priscilla   d. 1835   663   age 57
Dixon   Isaac F.   b. 3/22/1806   d. 1/5/1873   H118
Dixon   Elizabeth S.   b 2/9/1818   d. 1/23/1871   H119
Dixon   Robert   d. 6/4/1848   H127   age 28
Dixon   Elizabeth T   d. 4/14/1848   H126   age 28
Dixon   Kate Benteen   b. 11/16/1817   d. 1/16/1877   H128   wife of Isaac Jr., H121
Dixon   Isaac F. Jr.   b. 1/6/1841   d. 5/30/1878   H121   husband of Kate B., H128
Dixon   William H.   H131
Dixon   John E.   H133
Dixon   Emma Sara Needles   b. 2/24/1860   d. 7/31/1953   H162 & H163
Dixon   William A.   b. 9/3/1874   d. 11/19/1941   H162 & H163
Dorsey   Dr. S. D.   d. 1850   F26
Dorsey   Lucy   b. 12/13/1812   d. 4/27/1899   F32
Dorsey   Dr. William T.   b. 6/4/1818   d. 4/15/1870   F33
Dukehart   Ann M.   d. 3/21/1842   618   age 12
Dukehart   Capt. Theodore E. d. 1/17/1848   619   age 59
Dukehart   Mary M.   d. 7/5/1827   G19   age 82
Dukehart   Ann P.   b. 7/26/1806   d. 4/18/1898   H191
Dukehart   John   d. 12/17/1878   H192   age 78
Dukehart   Anna   d. 3/28/1833   I262   age 15
Duncan   Edwin Funkhauser   b. 1/13/1908   d. 10/22/1967   C25   son of Dr. W. L. Duncan & Ida B. Ulbray
Duncan   Mary Tennyson   d. 7/18/1906   C26
Dunham   Ellen Ann   b. 3/8/1911   d. (alive)   A124
Dunham   Henry Brown   b. 8/3/1912   d. 9/23/1930   A125
Dunham   Margene H. Brown   b. 5/9/1885   d. 9/7/1949   A126

Dunham Warren Benyew b. 2/4/1863 d. 9/2/1941 A127

E

E. I. E. 628
E. M. d. 1809 652
E. E. d. 1826 655
E. P. P. d. 1868 F35 could be P. P. Ellicott
Eachus Joseph d. 12/25/1842 638 age 9
Edmondson Dr. Thomas E82
Elder child E118
Elder Carrie E119 no stone
Elder Rachel A. E119 no stone
Elder child E120 no stone
Elder Robert F. E121 no stone
Elder child E122 no stone
Elder Michael H. d. 9/24/1900 E127 age 74, no stone
Elder Eliza R. E127 no stone
Eldridge Sarah Ann b. 6/11/1816 d. 5/7/1896 B106
Eldridge Susan S. d. 2/21/1901 C50 age 73
Ellicott Maria d. 1839 F29 age 39
Ellicott P. P. F36 from 10a book
Etter Ruth Ashcom Hough b. 11/13/1898 d. 12/27/1987 A109 wife of John L., possibly A110
Etter John L. b. 10/15/1894 d. 10/14/1949 A109 husband of Ruth A.H., A109
Everett Eliza b. 8/31/1807 d. 3/22/1889 G71 daughter of George M. & Mary Marsh
Ewing Henry d. 4/11/1854 I96 age 74
Ewing Ann d. 8/5/1852 I97 age 74
Ewing J. I438 no stone, Webb lots

Farrington - fieldstone

Farrington   Jane C.   b. 1876   d. 11/27/1944   H90
Farrington   Christina   d. 1/16/1936   H91   age 85
Farrington   Edward H.   d. 7/2/1904   H91   age 15, son of Christina, H91
Fehrman   Charles G.   b. 1870   d. 2/28/1931   G36   age 60
Fenton   Virginia Thomas   b. 1860   d. 10/28/1929   E137   age 69, sister of Thaddeus Thomas
Ferris   Mary   d. 7/19/1849   H475
fieldstone   604
fieldstone   605
fieldstone   606
fieldstone   607
fieldstone   608
fieldstone   609
fieldstone   610
fieldstone   G73
fieldstone   G74
fieldstone   G75
fieldstone   H199
fieldstone   H319
fieldstone   H369
fieldstone   H370
fieldstone   H373
fieldstone   H413
fieldstone   H455
fieldstone   H459   owned by Baynes
fieldstone   H460   owned by Baynes
fieldstone   H461   owned by Baynes
fieldstone   H462   owned by Baynes
fieldstone   I291

fieldstone — *Fussell*

fieldstone H457 owned by Baynes
Fincher Maria Price b. 8/4/1801 d. 9/24/1892 I131 wife of Benjamin Fincher
Folk Ann d. 1844 I192
Foos Elizabeth A. d. 1905 I14 no stone
Foos William W. I66 no stone
Forbush Bliss Sr. b. 1/14/1896 d. 4/6/1987 A213
Forbush Laverne Hill b. 10/26/1894 d. 7/19/1990 A214
Forbush Gabrielle Elliott b. 6/28/1890 d. 5/30/1988 A215
Forbush Arthur Rex b. 6/29/1892 d. 2/25/1952 A216
Forbush Maude Barden b. 8/12/1868 d. 12/24/1951 A217
Forbush William Byron b. ?/1868 d. 10/23/1927 A218 father of Bliss Sr., A213
Foss Elizabeth A. d. 3/14/1905 I14 age 74
Foss William W. d. 5/6/1889 I66 married daughter of James M. Kerr? from 9b book
Fox Sarah b. 2/4/1810 d. 2/21/1890 G25E wife of Charles, G26E (G28E)
Fox Charles J. b. 9/?/1792 d. 9/?/1866 G26E husband of Sarah, G25E (G27E)
Fraser Georgianna Z. Mott b. 7/4/1834 d. 11/15/1893 H525 wife of Alexander
French Clementine A. b. 5/18/1837 d. 9/9/1857 E66
Fuller Joshua M. b. 11/30/1828 d. 7/2/1876 H537
Fullman Ella d. 10/07/1887 G43 age 28, not on stone
Fulton Franklin Davis b. 10/14/1897 d. 1/18/1980 A273
Fulton Charles Lee Jr. b. 11/16/1895 d. 10/5/1965 E205 from Howard County, Maryland
Fulton Maria Davis b. 12/26/1867 d. 8/2/1956 E206 from Richmond, Virginia
Fulton Charles Lee b. 12/3/1866 d. 9/1/1961 E207 from Howard County, Maryland
Fussell William d. 1834 635 age 19
Fussell Joshua d. 8/3/1896 I195 age 74, no stone
Fussell Clarissa d. 4/28/1863 I196

Fussell - Gauline

Fussell   B. Howard   d. 12/29/1860   I197   age 37
Fussell   Edwin M.   d. 7/19/1851   I198
Fussell   Jacob   d. 1862   I199

G

G. M.   E217   Gray?
Gardner   William G.   d. 8/12/1879   C49   age 17
Gardner   Alfred S.   b. 2/2/1821   d. 3/19/1906   C51
Gardner   Mary Elma   d. 12/15/1872   C52   age 42
Gardner   Nancy Taylor   b. 11/25/1831   d. 3/18/1917   C61
Gardner   James   b. 8/19/1818   d. 3/29/1881   C62
Gardner   J. Herbert   b. 7/11/1869   d. 1/20/1879   C63   son of James & Nancy, C61/C62
Gardner   Elizabeth (Lizzie) T.   b. 8/19/1861   d. 7/11/1876   C64   daughter of James & Nancy, C61/C62
Gardner   Sarah G.   b. 6/30/1855   d. 7/9/1876   C65   daughter of James & Nancy, C61/C62
Gardner   Ephraim   d. 5/?/1869   I71   age 81, father of Alfred, C51
Gardner   Mary   d. 12/19/1867   I72   age 70
Gardner   Martha S.   d. 1861   I73   unreadable stone
Garwood   Margaretta L.   b. 3/13/1816   d. 9/4/1887   F133   daughter of Jonathan & Elizabeth Beans, wife of Clayton, F134
Garwood   Clayton   b. 8/4/1822   d. 3/11/1888   F134   son of Garwood & Mary Scott
Gatchell   Mary Elizabeth   d. 8/31/1950   K13   age 61, in Lamb plot
Gauline   Mary Elizabeth   d. 4/26/1900   F107
Gauline   Dr. James R.   F108
Gauline   Charles D.   F109
Gauline   Annie R.   F110
Gauline   Mary A.   d. 7/31/1889   F111   age 72
Gauline   Catherine E.   d. 9/18/1923   F112   age 72

Gauline - Gilpin

Gauline   John B.   F113
Gebb   Mary B.   d. 3/3/1893   C79   age 79, wife of Henry, C82
Gebb   William T.   d. 11/8/1880   C80   age 26
Gebb   George O.   d. 10/4/1880   C81   age 28
Gebb   Henry   d. 1/2/1899   C82   age 69, husband of Mary B., C79
Geddes   Susan S.   d. 12/27/1890   sister of Ann Maria Birdsall Cobb
Geist   George E.   d. 10/22/1875   H8   age 35
George   Sarah   d. 1829   676
Giese   Sarah N.   b. 5/18/1818   d. 10/27/1904   B14
Gilbreath   Erasmus G.   b. 1787   d. 1870   B126 in #14 book as died 1876
Giles   Miriam   b. 9/12/1814   d. 12/17/1869   I91
Gillingham   John S.   d. 7/28/1836   631   age 9 m.
Gillingham   Capt. Christopher R.   b. ?/2/1844   d. 12/16/1911   E54   husband of Sellona M., E95
Gillingham   Sellonna M.   b. 9/14/1857   d. 3/22/1911   E95   wife of Christopher R., E54
Gillingham   Christopher B.   b. 1/8/1888   d. 12/19/1904   E96
Gillingham   Catherine B.   b. 2/3/1814   d. 6/19/1894   E98
Gillingham   Edward E.   b. 4/16/1816   d. 8/12/1873   E99   age 57
Gillingham   Albert Pecare   d. 2/9/ 1902   E100   age 6 w., child of William R., no stone.
Gillingham   child   E101   no stone
Gillingham   child   E102   no stone
Gillingham   Edward E. Jr.   d. 12/7/1890   E103   age 51
Gillingham   Edward E.   d. 12/7/1887   E103   age 2 m. possibly child in E101, son of William R.
Gillingham   F97 sister-in-law of R. Gillingham from 10a book
Gillingham   William R. Jr.   d. 12/11/1892   H446   age $3^{1}/_{2}$ m., no stone
Gillingham   Mary   d. 2/13/1850   I133   age 63
Gillingham   John   d. 6/11/1818   I134   age 61
Gilpin   Bernard Jr.   b. 9/7/1855   d. 3/1/1914   A166
Gilpin   Helen Spillane   d. 3/27/1946   A166   age 86
Gilpin   Mary B.   b. 7/5/1834   d. 6/21/1906   A167
Gilpin   Bernard Sr.   b. 3/6/1826   d. 5/7/1897   A168

Gilpin - Green

Gilpin James S. d. 6/26/1851 I157 age 31
Gilpin Thomas Henry d. 1/4/1854 I158 age 23
Glenn Eleanor Trump b. 7/30/1842 d. 6/14/1922 H404
Glenn Elizabeth Sewall b. 6/22/1881 d. 3/18/1971 H451 buried with Charles A. & Marie L. Lasar, not on stone
Goulding Helen L. Plummer d. 11/22/1959 H19 age 89, not on stone, see Philip S. Plummer
Goulding Philip S. b. 9/6/1876 d. 5/10/1937 H19 Plummer?
Gover Cornelia b. 4/21/1823 d. 2/10/1904 F5
Graham Elizabeth T. b. 10/11/1858 d. 10/17/1920 A189 listed on permit as A252
Graham John T. b. 12/4/1833 d. 2/15/1923 A190
Grahame Beulah A. d. 1843 I11 no stone
Grahame George d. 8/23/1851 I59
Grahame Thomas J. d. 1854? I62 age 27 death 9-25-18?
Gray Wilhelmina b. 1797 d. 1862 E221
Gray Dr. Watson Womach b. 10/5/1892 d. 8/29/1960 K35
Gray George b. 1801 d. 1883 E241
Gray Mary Ann b. 12/11/1821 d. 3/14/1913 E238
Gray Dorothy Davis K34 wife of Watson W., K35
Gray Corilla b. 1799 d. 1874 E216
Gray George P. b. 1827 d. 1851 E220
Green Mary Edith d. 1/16/1907 B56 age 41, no stone
Green children E233 of John N., E235
Green Richard C. d. 3/24/1890 E234 age 89
Green John N. Jr. E235
Green H. G80
Green Mary d. 9/1/1852 H138 age 76
Green Susan C. b. 7/3/1805 d. 1/11/1892 I343 wife of Richard, I344
Green Richard C. b. 8/31/1860 d. 3/24/1890 I344 unsure of birth year, husband of Susan C., I343
Green John N. I345
Green J. A. I346
Green Charles A. I348 unreadable stone

Green   child   I350   no stone
Green   child   I351   no stone
Green   R. W.   I352   no stone

H

H. M. E.   646
Haines   Elizabeth R.   b. 8/4/1836   d. 8/29/1917   H565
Hall   Mary Ellen Garwood   b. 7/29/1857   d. 2/17/1932   F134½
Hall   Newton Taylor   b. 6/12/1857   d. 10/10/1894   F135
Hall   Gerald G.   b. 11/16/1888   d. 9/21/1934   F136
Hall   Enola Margaretta   b. 8/2/1891   d. 6/28/1987   F137
Halwadt   Rebecca   d. 11/5/1894   H268   age 75, twin daughter of Charles & Sarah, H271/H272
Halwadt   Sarah   d. 8/3/1894   H269   age 75, twin daughter of Charles & Sarah, H271/H272
Halwadt   Elizabeth   d 7/17/1883   H270   daughter of Charles & Sarah, H271/H272
Halwadt   Sarah   d. 8/03/1873   H271   age 86
Halwadt   Charles   d. 9/17/1860   H272   age 81
Handy   Elizabeth Ann   b. 1823   d. 1835   H287   age 12
Handy   Elizabeth   d. 9/?/1840   H341   age 50?
Handy   Sallie C.   d. 8/8/1888   H343   age 70, wife of Jesse, H344
Handy   Dr. Jesse T.   b. 8/17/1813   d. 3/31/1885   H344   husband of Sallie, H343
Handy   Dr. W. W.   d. 1/27/1864   H345   age 79
Handy   Sallie C.   H347   unreadable stone, name from #14 book
Hanson   Elizabeth R.   b. 1823   d. 1873   H167
Hanson   Mary B.   d. 11/27/1870   H168
Hanson   Thomas P.   d. 6/11/1845   I77   age 59
Hanson   Mary P.   d. 6/29/1849   I78   age 64
Hanson   John P.   I80   unreadable stone

Hanson - Hartley

Hanson   Louisa S.   d. 11/6/1875   I84   age either 10 or 40
Hanson   J. Poultney   d. 8/18/1881   I85   age 21
Hardesty   Sarah C.   d. 3/10/1916   E87   no stone
Harlan   Flora B.   b. 1906   d. 1/7/1970   A123
Harlan   Joseph   b. 1909   d. 1985   A123   on map as died 1970
Harlan   Enoch H.   b. 1867   d. 5/2/1941   A123   age 73 y. 6 m.
Harlan   Mary Benson   b. 1873   d. 4/9/1957   A123
Harlan   Samuel   d. 1850   I76
Harper   Cornelia Albertson   b. 1833   d. 3/16/1910   E62   wife of John S., E63
Harper   John Sylvester   d. 1/13/1892   E63   age 59   husband of Cornelia A., E62
Harris   Samuel Murry   d. 2/10/1885   H531   unsure of date   husband of Guilielma M., H533
Harris   Guilielma Mott   d. 8/5/1870   H533   age 51?   wife of Samuel M., H531
Harris   Mrs. George   I52   no stone
Harris   George M.D.   b. 12/28/1797   d. 2/9/1872   I53
Harris   Hicks   b. 11/3/1802   d. 4/26/1866   I54
Harris   Margarate H.   d. 2/20/1863   I55   age 48
Harrod   Eliza   I124   no stone
Harry   Elizabeth E.   b. 11/12/1875   d. 10/24/1972   A195
Harry   James Warner   b. 3/20/1870   11/13/1948   A196   also listed as James Warner White
Hartley   Wilber T. (G.)   b. 1/7/1875   d. 4/4/1948   C19
Hartley   Emily J.   b. 7/26/1880   d. 1/8/1930   C20
Hartley   James Manning   b. 8/25/1888   d. 3/31/1895   C22   son of Joseph H. & Elizabeth A., C23/C24
Hartley   child   C22   of Joseph
Hartley   Elizabeth A. (Lizzie)   b. 1/18/1859   d. 6/30/1913   C23   "mother"
Hartley   Joseph H.   b. 4/17/1857   d. 9/17/1928   C24   "father"
Hartley   Wilber F.   C119   from 10a book
Hartley   Bertha Cain   b. 4/19/1874   d. 7/22/1957   H433
Hartley   Samuel E.   b. 12/8/1864   d. 2/5/1941   H434

Hartley - Holloway

Hartley Anna E. b. 12/2/1866 d. 10/30/1942 H437 daughter of Phineas & Deborah, H438/439
Hartley Deborah A. b. 12/11/1828 d. 6/17/1920 H438
Hartley Phineas T. b. 9/11/1824 d. 3/5/1894 H439 son of Thomas
Hartley Martha P. b. 6/18/1826 d. 12/11/1888 I33
Hartley Elias P. b. 4/23/1821 d. 5/26/1883 I331/2
Hartley unmarked C21 from 10a book
Haulton Mary B. d. 1847 I274 age 89
Haviland Betsey S. b. 1/25/1820 d. 5/13/1893 G91
Haviland Ebenezer W. b. 6/11/1819 d. 6/23/1887 G92
Hawley Mary b. 8/10/1791 d. 7/4/1872 G30
Hayward George C. d. 7/3/1870 E2 age 65
Hayward Elizabeth d. 1/10/1871 E3 age 76
Hayward Margaretta d. 3/5/1847 232 age 24
Henry Mark Harris d. 1/16/1850 I58 age 5
Hibbard Edward J. b. 2/22/1847 d. 3/3/1927 I312
Hibberd Royden J. b. 10/27/1883 d. 11/6/1889 G70
Hibberd James M. b. 4/10/1801 d. 12/1/1883 I310
Hibberd Mary R. d. 9/30/1894 I311 age 84, no stone
Hill Ann d. 1804 658
Hill Mary I490 field stone
Hirsch Matthew Hessberg b. 1909 d. 1983 F18 should be K18 by records on cards
Hishmeh Sabha Sueliman b. 3/8/1900 d. 10/2/1981 E163 listed on map as Sueliman, E164
Holland Mary Johnson b. 1/20/1894 d. 3/24/1979 K26 possibly C100
Hollingsworth Norman Berry b. 1924 d. 1983 A246
Hollingsworth Edna L. Hull b. 1/2/1887 d. 8/12/1970 B23 on burial certificate as B24
Hollingsworth Clement W. b. 1889 d. 11/22/1946 B24 age 57, listed in 1931 book as Camilla Wright Robinson
Holloway Edward d. 1/20/1866 H299 age 10
Holloway Ellen H. d. 11/2/1874 H300 age 82

Holloway - Hopkins

Holloway Robert d. 7/20/1863 H301 age 77
Holloway Alexander d. 5/15/1916 H302 age 84
Holloway Mary Jane d. 9/23/1919 H303 age 89
Holme Hilda P. d. 3/6/1960 A128 age 71, no stone
Holme Henry D. b. 4/23/1887 d. 12/11/1924 A129
Holme Anne W. b. 9/9/1884 d. 12/11/1924 A130
Holme Pauline W. b. 11/12/1848 d. 6/14/1940 A131
Holme Richard Henry b. 12/17/1849 d. 4/22/1921 A132
Holt Gertrude b. 7/5/1875 d. 1/17/1951 I411
Holt Chalkley b. 1835 d. 5/29/1920 I412 husband of Rachel R., I413
Holt Rachel R. b. 1840 d. 3/4/1905 I413 wife of Chalkley
Hoopes Adelia b. 12/25/1811 d. 7/17/1892 age 75, daughter of Amos & Edith M., 9b from 1892 minutes
Hoopes Elizabeth Coroman b. /17/1818 d. 5/19/1884 B96 daughter of Davis H., B99
Hoopes Walter Ernest b. 12/29/1859 d. 5/29/1889 B97 drowned at Johnstown, Pennsylvania. (Johnstown flood) with 2 sons (memorial stone)
Hoopes Davis Haines b. 7/15/1803 d. 7/17/1873 B99
Hoopes Phoebe Churchman d. 1/11/1887 B100 age 7 m. 7 d.
Hoopes Mary H. d. 7/26/1843 H110 age 10, from P.C. book bought by Florence Hoopes
Hoopes Amos b. 6/30/1773 d. 9/2/1865 I34 91 y. 2 m. 2nd husband of Edith M., I35 on stone as Hoops
Hoopes Edith Matlack d. 11/30/1857 I35 age 83, consort of Amos, I36
Hopkins Mary Elizabeth 657 age 3
Hopkins Elizabeth W. b. 9/11/1875 d. 10/10/1960 A94 daughter of William E. Walton
Hopkins Charles B143 no stone
Hopkins Sophia d. 7/13/1887 E172 age 86
Hopkins Charlotte W. d. 12/31/1871 E173 age 76
Hopkins Elizabeth Walton d. 10/10/1960 F58 age 85, from 1931 book; daughter of William E. Walton, 9b
Hopkins Josefa N. (M.) Crosby b. 8/5/1833 d. 2/6/1930 F61 wife of Roger B., F62 (F60)

Hopkins Roger Brooke b. 2/2/1864 d. 8/16/1927 F62 husband of Josefa N.C., F61
Hopkins Elizabeth J. b. 7/14/1852 d. 4/12/1935 F62½ daughter of Gerard T. & Elizabeth R.
Hopkins Gerard T. Jr. b. 12/24/1861 d. 12/12/1918 F63
Hopkins Gerard T. b. 10/10/1816 d. 10/10/1900 F64
Hopkins Elizabeth R. b. 10/10/1823 d. 10/23/1896 F65
Hopkins Frank N. b. 1818 d. 1879 F67
Hopkins Richard S. b. 12/26/1790 d. 8/2/1872 H21
Hopkins Sarah S. b. 4/16/1793 d. 4/7/1871 H22
Hopkins John C. (L.) d. 12/17/1848 H128 age 3
Hopkins Sarah Ann d. 6/12/1848 H129 age 4
Hopkins Elizabeth d. 1/20/1832 H217 age 60
Hopkins Johns d. 8/28/1837 H218 age 74
Hopkins Richard P. d. 5/23/1842 H342 age 32
Hopkins Annette B. b. 10/18/1879 d. 5/14/1970 H355 daughter of Luther W., H359, & Katherine B.
Hopkins John Howard b. 5/10/1882 d. 2/18/1952 H357
Hopkins Sarah Catherine b. 12/16/1841 d. 12/26/1928 H358
Hopkins Luther W. b. 11/13/1843 d. 7/2/1920 H359
Hopkins Helen C. d. 4/23/1886 H360 age 2 y. 3 m.
Hopkins George d. 10/31/1861 H452 age 69
Hopkins Ann Eliza d. 12/13/1890 H468 age 70, daughter of Richard & Mary Ann Gover, no stone
Hopkins Susan d. 3/10/1865 H557 age 80
Hopkins Rachel b. 5/19/1822 d. 5/17/1891 H559
Hopkins Elizabeth b. 3/31/1802 d. 12/09/1890 H560 daughter of Richard & Mary Annover
Hopkins Thomas d. 2/17/1886 H561 age 75
Hopkins William d. 5/28/1881 H562 age 67
Hopkins Dorothy d. 12/15/1857 H563 age 81
Hough Marietta Sophia d. 10/28/1893 age 82
Houlton Mary 1274 from 10a book
Howard Eliza d. 1844 H200

Howland - Hunter

Howland	Daniel	I386
Hughes	Sarah	d. 11/5/1877 B46 age 70 y. 9 m. 17 d.
Hughes	William H.	d. 9/27/1907 B47 age 65 y. 5 m. 8 d.
Hughes	James A.	b. 1835 d. 1/28/1922 B48
Hughes	Elizabeth J.	b. 1839 d. 11/20 1922 B49 age 83½
Hughes	Francis	b. 1838 d. 5/30/1927 B50
Hughes	John Thomas	b. 7/15/1827 d. 9/24/1890 I19
Hughes	Annie P.	b. 8/13/1841 d. 2/15/1873 I20
Hughes	George	b. 8/19/1844 d. 6/2/1863 I22
Hull	Mary Katherine Doster b. 11/5/1898 d. 8/27/1963 B92 wife of Robert Franklin	
Hull	Thomas Jackson F85 in memory of ?	
Hull	Harriet Coale Ford F85 in memory of ?	
Hull	Caroline R. d. 5/5/1913 F87 age 70, wife of William S., F88	
Hull	William Skipwith d. 7/13/1909 F88 age 87, husband of Caroline, F87	
Hull	Mary Dixon b. 12/5/1840 d. 10/15/1924 H112 wife of Thomas B., H113	
Hull	Thomas Burling b. 10/31/1834 d. 2/2/1906 H113 husband of Mary D., H112	
Hull	Almira A. b. 7/23/1881 d. 1/23/1900 H114 "our Alma"	
Hull	Robert B. b. 8/3/1866 d. 9/29/1890 H115 "our oldest son"	
Hull	Charles Abel b. 11/19/1868 d. 2/21/1871 H116	
Hull	Helen P. Lamb b. 1/29/1875 d. 7/2/1969 J44 wife of Thomas B. Jr., J45, daughter of Eli M. Lamb & Anna W. Cochran, I40/I41	
Hull	Thomas Burling Jr. b. 8/3/1873 d. 8/21/1934 J45 husband of Helen P., J44	
Hull	Mary Bromwell b. 6/29/1872 d. 8/31/1946 J49	
Hull	James Dixon b. 10/9/1872 d. 1/21/1950 J50	
Hull	Randolph M. b. 10/19/1904 d. 5/20/1983 J57	
Hull	Marie (Maxie) Herring b. 9/14/1899 d. 6/11/1974 J58 "Mexie"	
Hull	Sadie Randolph b. 9/30/1870 d. 4/3/1955 J59	
Hull	John Burling b. 7/17/1869 d. 6/9/1936 J60	
Hunter	Edward P. b. 11/1/1891 d. 8/25/1895 C57 son of James	

Hunter - Janney

Hunter   Thomas P.   b. 2/19/1892   d. 7/31/1898   C58   son of James & Zora
Hunter   Zora Elizabeth Pardoe   b. 1867   d. 3/19/1939   C59   age 72 y. 4 m., wife of Thomas J., C60
Hunter   Thomas James   b. 1/3/1865   d. 8/6/1940   C60   husband of Zora E., C59
Hunton   Grace V.   b. 9/25/1881   d. 9/6/1948   I2   no stone
Hunton   Rachel Mott   d. 2/19/1920   I3   age 72
Husband   Jacob L.   d. 6/4/1901   H240
Husband   Margaret T.   d. 10/12/1896   H241   age 59
Husband   Mary B.   H275   age 70

I

I. I.   H284   no stone

J

J. G. F.   d. 1829   H252
Jacklay   Francis Dano   b. 1/22/1900   d. 1/10/1967   A271
Jackson   Emilie Painter   d. 10/26/1918   E159   age 78, daughter of Edwin Painter
Jackson   2 children & Frank P.   d. 1887/89/90   H328   children of Ralph & Mary Webster Jackson, no stone
Jackson   Emilie P.   d. 5/3/1888   H329   age 24 y. 9 m., daughter of Ralph & Mary Webster Jackson
Jackson   Edgar   d. 8/1/1938   H329½   age 45
James   Ann   E47   from 10a book
James   Amos   H414   unreadable stone
Janney   Ellen   d. 5/6/1887   B10   age 65, daughter of Jacob & Elizabeth H.

Janney - Jones

Janney   Henry   b. 4/27/1811   d. 11/7/1895   B12
Janney   Hannah R.   b. 9/7/1816   d. 7/21/1908   B13
Janney   M. Elizabeth   b. 7/14/1843   d. 2/1/1927   B15   daughter of Henry & Hannah R., B12/B13
Janney   Hannah Hopkins   b. 1/5/1852   d. 10/25/1930   B16
Janney   Bertha   d. 5/13/1955   B17   age 84
Janney   Joseph J.   d. 11/30/1920   B18   age 79
Janney   Anna Townsend   d. 2/26/1891   B18   age 47
Janney   Martha (Mattie) T.   b. 6/15/1876   d. 7/1/1877   B19   daughter of Anna T. & Joseph J., B18
Janney   Esther S.   b. 11/30/1841   d. 1/3/1926   B137
Janney   Dr. Edwin W.   b. 6/30/1837   d. 11/28/1923   B138
Janney   Lucy K.   d. 12/15/1880   B139   7 m.
Janney   Arthur C.   d. 4/29/1871   B140   16 m.
Janney   Annie C.   d. 11/11/1868   B141   6 m.
Janney   Dr. Oliver Edward   b. 3/8/1856   d. 11/17/1930   E21
Janney   Anne Webb   b. 7/8/1861   d. 1/30/1933   E22
Janney   William Webb   b. 10/30/1890   d. 10/30/1890   E23   son of Oliver & Anne, E21/E22
Janney   Phida   d. 1/3/1964   K8   age 80, listed in 1931 book as K6
Janney   Elizabeth H. Brooks   d. 8/6/1919   K9   age 63 1/2, wife of William. H., K10
Janney   William Henry   d. 3/6/1935   K10   age 84 3/4, husband of Elizabeth H., K9
Jeffries   Lydia   d. 9/17/1877   H265   age 90, grandmother of Lydia C. Stables, H264
Johns   Stephen   I461
Johnson   Emma Schooley   d. 1/18/1935   C90   age 68 y. 7 m. 6 d. wife of Robert G
Johnson   Hannah   d. 8/30/1892   C98   age 3 d., "little sister"
Johnson   Eliza   d. 5/26/1847   I280
Jolliffe   Margaret Hopkins   b. 8/26/1819   d. 10/9/1898   H558
Jones   Samuel G.   d. 1842   654   age 64
Jones   C.   d. 1835   664

Jones   Charles Howard   d. 9/7/1878   C34   age 28 y. 10 m.
Jones   Morris Davis   d. 12/5/1878   C35   age 18, son of John & Caroline, C36/C37
Jones   John   b. 7/2/1877   d. 8/11/1887   C36
Jones   Caroline M.   b. 11/4/1824   d. 4/12/1909   C37
Jones   James   b. 4/14/1844   d. 5/2/1921   E212
Jones   Mary Talbot   b. 10/1/1828   d. 2/12/1921   E213
Jones   James   d. 11/29/1880   E214   age 78 y. 8 m.
Jones   Elizabeth   d. 8/28/1876   E215   age 73
Jones   Sarah J.   d. 8/26/1819   E218   age 16 y. 2 m.
Jones   John P.   b. 2/5/1826   d. 1/25/1853   E219
Jones   Charles H.   d. 12/17/1866   E222   age 26 y. 6 m.
Jones   Virginia B.   b. 12/17/1862   d. 3/5/1927   E239   age 65
Jones   Henry G.   b. 12/18/1830   d. 10/29/1901   E240
Jones   Fannie   b. 8/?/1795   d. 3/19/1815   H507
Jones   Ann   b. 6/29/1810   d. 6/25/1826   H507   daughter of Fannie
Jones   Nicholas S.   d. 1858   H508   unreadable stone
Jones   John Brown   d. 5/11/1872   H509   unsure of date

K

K.   C. V.   d. 1831   I407
Kemp   Ellen   b. 1/16/1798   d. 10/10/1865   E148
Kemp   John W.   d. 9/10/1837   H290
Kemp   Sarah E.   d. 3/2/1838   H292
Kerr   Samuel   d. 3/20/1893   G40   age 63, husband of Susannah, G41, no stone
Kerr   Susannah   d. 3/12/1891   G41   age 67, wife of Samuel, G40
Kerr   James M.   b. 7/12/1855   d. 12/25/1891   G43
King   Bertha E.   b. 1897   d. 6/12/1955   A122   age 76
King   Jessie L.   b. 1881   d. 3/25/1956   A122   age 82
Kinsey   O. Jr.   d. 1832   I313
Kinsey   S. G.   d. 1831   I367

Kirk - Lamb

Kirk James H. d. 1859 I380
Kirk Albina P. b. 10/28/1796 d. 12/23/1865 I382
Kirk Samuel b. 2/15/1793 d. 7/6/1872 I383
Knight Elizabeth M. b. 12/16/1815 d. 10/15/1880 E24 daughter of Isaac & Julianna M., I153/I154
Knight Ann Rebecca b. 11/11/1822 d. 11/8/1880 E25 daughter of Isaac & Julianna M., I153/I154
Knight Mary V. b. 11/14/1826 d. 4/13/1903 E26 daughter of Isaac & Julianna M., I153/I154
Knight John B. b. 6/2/1811 d. 12/31/1897 I67
Knight John d. 5/20/1863 I68
Knight Mira d. 6/16/1857 I128
Knight Julianna Maria b. 1/16/1795 d. 2/20/1868 I153
Knight Isaac I154
Knight Granville S. I156 unreadable stone
Knight S. B. d. 12/8/1842 I191
Knight William H. d. 10/?/1847 I204 age 26
Knight Charles A. d. 7/12/1848 I207 age 35
Knox Mary 667 age 15

L

L. R. M. 633
Laferta P. H. d. 1847 H278
Laferta Jacob d. 1849 H279
Laferta W. C. H280
Lafetra Jane B. d. 8/1/1889 H276 age 73
Lafetra Phoebe E. d. 1855 H277
Lamb Phillip Edward b. 1884 d. 4/7/1963 C125
Lamb Marjory Mathews b. 1885 d. 1984 C125
Lamb Rachel E. b. 5/13/1845 d. 1/28/1933 E179 daughter of John E. & Esther Lamb

Lamb - Larrabee

Lamb Louise Emerson b. 3/28/1859 d. 4/29/1926 F105 wife of John Emerson, F106
Lamb John Emerson b. 1852 d. 7/21/1890 F106 husband of Louise E., F105
Lamb Louise Emerson b. 1890 d. 1983 F106 daughter of John E. & Louise E., F105/F106
Lamb Annie R. b. 1/13/1850 d. 1/5/1933 H569
Lamb George M. b. 7/25/1847 d. 1/2/1908 H570
Lamb George M. Jr. b. 9/4/1879 d. 1/31/1957 H571
Lamb Eli Matthews b. 11/14/1835 d. 1/25/1911 I40 husband of Anna W., I41
Lamb Anna W. (Cochran?) b. 12/27/1839 d. 11/4/1929 I41 wife of Eli M., I40
Lamb Mary Elizabeth b. 1/29/1875 d. 7/4/1970 I42 sister of Helen Lamb Hull, J44
Lamb Margaretta Walton b. 12/19/1880 d. 6/9/1972 I43 daughter of Eli M. Lamb & Anna W. Corkran (Cochran), I40/I41
Lamborn I. S. 649 age 29
Lamborn William G54 no stone
Lamborn Mary R. d. 12/22/1933 K14 age 81
Lamborn Louis d. 11/16/1926 K15 age 69
Lamburn Sr. d. 1850 650 age 74
Lancaster Richard P. H15 from 10a book
Larrabee Elizabeth H. b. 11/26/1807 d. 5/11/1876 B85
Larrabee William b. 2/23/1811 d. 2/4/1892 B86
Larrabee D. G. d. 4/22/1868 I81
Larrabee E. M. d. 11/17/1870 I82
Larrabee Joseph M. d. 1/29/1849 I135 age 33
Larrabee Daniel d. 9/11/1812 I137 age 72
Larrabee Anna d. 1855 I138 age 76
Larrabee Joseph Oliver d. 6/13/1849 I139 age 6
Larrabee Hannah S. d. 11/13/1849 I140 age 3
Larrabee Robert Gover d. 8/16/1851 I141 age 15 m.
Larrabee Howard Potter d. 6/10/1853 I142 18 m.

Larrabee - Lovejoy

Larrabee Eleanor Spindler d. 8/17/1856   I143
Larrabee E. W. d. 9/10/1858   I144
Larrabee Elizabeth A. d. 12/30/1891   I145   age 82
Lee Mary R. Webster d. 8/19/1914   H331   age 51, wife of Herbert W.
Lee Hannah Ann Tyson b. 2/22/1856 d. 1/26/1932   H544   wife of Columbus O'Donnel Lee
Leek Rebecca M. d. 8/?/1807   662   age 7 m.
Lesar Charles A. b. 2/8/1856 d. 1/08/1936   H451
Lesar Marie Louise b. 10/5/1848 d. 1/6/1946   H451
Lester Mary d. 1850   673   age 79
Lewis Grace Winder b. 4/25/1881 d. 11/28/1963   A139   wife of Herbert S., A140
Lewis Herbert S. b. 2/9/1880 d. 7/20/1971   A140   husband of Grace, A139
Lewis Annie b. 9/11/1862 d. 2/15/1937   C83   wife of Charles, C84
Lewis Charles W. b. 5/10/1853 d. 12/30/1917   C84   husband of Annie, C83
Lewis Alice J. b. 12/13/1897 d. 3/18/1897   C85   child of Charles, C84
Lewis infant b. 10/26/1916 d. 10/26/1916   C85   child of Carroll Lewis
Lewis Walter D. b. 6/4/1879 d. 6/11/1910   C86   "son"
Lewis Annie L. b. 12/26/1853 d. 1/19/1926   C104
Lewis Louis b. 3/17/1852 d. 3/3/1911   C105
Lewis Virginia b. 10/2/1845 d. 12/24/1911   C106
Lewis Ellen b. 4/19/1817 d. 7/12/1902   C107
Lewis Frank S. G20   no stone
Lewis Louis d. 3/3/1911   I31   age 59, no stone
Lexington John d. 2/27/1838   624   age 73
Livingston Ann S. I223
Long Jesse Tyson b. 12/13/1867 d. 09/27/1899   H539
Lovegrove Rachel M. I24   no stone
Lovejoy Rebecca T. Albertson b. 1823 d. 8/15/1905   E64   wife of Perley R., E65
Lovejoy Perley R. d. 10/22/1889   E 65   age 68, husband of Rebecca T., E64

Lowery   Eliza T.   b. 2/4/1809   d. 2/13/1872   G48
Lutz   Grace Eliza   b. 9/13/1869   d. 5/28/1957   J1
Lutz   John P.   b. 8/24/1871   d. 11/13/1950   J2
Lyon   Anna M.   d. 1832   679

M   A E.   611
M   A.   d. 1817   623
Mackenzie   Cassandra Ann   b. 7/19/1854   d. 5/26/1945   E73   daughter of Thomas & Eleanora I., E79/E80
Mackenzie   Mary Eliza Taylor   b. 2/16/1853   d. 5/31/1935   E74   daughter of Thomas & Eleanora I., E79/E80.
Mackenzie   Dr. Edward Everett   b. 8/19/1858   d. 2/11/1928   E75
Mackenzie   Thomas   b. 11/1/1856   d. 9/8/1927   E76
Mackenzie   Colin Burgess   b. 4/3/1834   d. 10/27/1904   E77   3rd son of Thomas & Stacy Norbury Mackenzie
Mackenzie   Cosmo Taylor   d. 11/3/1902   E78   2nd son of Thomas & Stacy Norbury Mackenzie
Mackenzie   Eleanor Isabella   b. 4/4/1818   d. 11/9/1880   E79   wife of Thomas, E80
Mackenzie   Thomas   b. 3/20/1791   d. 6/2/1866   E80   husband of Eleanor I, E79, born in Calvert County, Maryland
Mackenzie   B. Tacy   d. 2/20/1837   E81   age 37 y. 8 m. 11 d.
Magness   Charles I.   b. 1865   d. 8/21/1941   H267   husband of Hannah M., H267
Magness   Hannah Messersmith   b. 3/19/1865   d. 3/23/1943   H267   age 78 y. 4 d., wife of Charles I., H267
Markley   Sauil A.   d. 1/24/1898   I86   age 53 from 9b book, could be Samuel
Markley   Samuel S.   b. 3/10/1845   d. 1/24/1898   I86
Markley   Grace A.   b. 2/19/1845   d. 3/2/1915   I86
Markley   Lillian L.   b. 7/6/1898   d. 10/15/1974   I89
Markley   Lillian L.   I90   same as I89 ?

Markley - Matthews

Markley Augusta A. b. 1/28/1871 d. 10/13/1941 I149
Markley Jacob S. b. 9/25/1870 d. 11/17/1926 I150
Marley Annie d. 6/13/1872 H54 age 21 y. 4 m., daughter of John & Maria, H55
Marley Maria d. 11/18/1901 H55 age 83
Marsh R. G84 no stone
Marsh Eliza d. 4/4/1857 H374
Marsh Hannah d. 3/5/1879 H375 age 85
Marsh Hannah d. 1846 H415
Marsh John d. 1845 H417
Martenet Maria Eva Eldridge b. 9/28/1916 d. 12/15/1992 J8 wife of Oscar III
Martenet Oscar C. Jr. b. 12/24/1889 d. 10/9/1925 J10
Martin Eleanora d. 1834 637 age 26
Martin Susannah d. 1842 656 age 82
Martin Mary b. 4/3/1792 d. 3/10/1871 G50
Mason Mary E. b. 1902 d. 1977 A50 Sexton & Caretaker; could be A51
Mason Ralph b. 1894 d. 1981 A73 Sexton & Caretaker; actually A52
Matthews John T. d. 7/12/1893 1893 minutes
Matthews William Whitelock d. 1/30/1899 age 56 from permit, body returned to Baltimore County, Maryland
Matthews Josephine d. 2/25/1905 age 55 from 1905 minutes
Matthews John T. d. 8/25/1903 from 1903 minutes
Matthews Ann d. 1/18 1849 617 age 89
Matthews Oliver J. b. 1863 d. 8/1/1947 C9 age 85
Matthews Laura S. b. 1867 d. 12/12/1953 C9a
Matthews Margaret Woolston d. 2/15/1930 C120 age 72
Matthews Charles T. d. 3/5/1937 C121 age 85
Matthews T. Stockton d. 1/15/1958 C122 age 76
Matthews C. Leigh b. 8/29/1882 d. 2/17/1952 C123 age 69
Matthews Elizabeth S. (M.) b. 10/5/1858 d. 6/13/1899 C130
Matthews Joseph B. M.D. b. 3/18/1855 d. 2/2/1888 C131 son of Joshua & Elizabeth Fuller Mott

Matthews - Matthews

Matthews Joshua T. b. 8/9/1881 d. 11/5/1882 C132
Matthews Thomas R. Jr. d. 1/15/1897 E169 age 66, stone missing or buried
Matthews Susan R. b. 10/18/1831 d. 8/26/1900 E170
Matthews Sarah Riley b. 2/10/1853 d. 12/2/1910 F45
Matthews Ann J. b. 1800 d. 1877 F68
Matthews Ann Eliza d. 2/14/1895 F103 age 73, wife of Thomas H.
Matthews Thomas R. d. 1/15/1898 F104 age 66, unsure of grave site 9b book
Matthews Mordecai H. d. 5/7/1867 H66 age 22, son of Mordecai H. & Philena E., H67/68
Matthews Philena E. d. 10/3/1878 H67 age 67, wife of Mordecai H., H68
Matthews Mordecai H d. 6/9/1873 H68 age 76, husband. of Philena, H67
Matthews Alfred H. d. 8/2/1880 H69 age 43
Matthews Mary Anna d. 10/20/1921 H70 age 74
Matthews Virginia J. d. 8/5/1911 H70 age 79
Matthews Richard J. b. 7/6/1831 d. 4/8/1885 H87
Matthews Richard J. d. 4/7/1897 H87 age 3 w., son of Richard J. Jr.
Matthews Sallie Scott b. 1/25/1830 d. 10/23/1885 H88
Matthews Thomas R. b. 12/27/1792 d. 9/2/1873 H108
Matthews Rachel d. 4/9/1869 H109
Matthews two children H130 no stone
Matthews E. Scott d. 3/16/1866 H132
Matthews Harry d. 7/12/1867 H134
Matthews Thomas R. b. 3/11/1863 d. 3/29/1865 H136 son of Richard S. & Sallie T.
Matthews E. H151 found on 3x5 card
Matthews Helen Lewis b. 10/22/1898 d. 11/5/1966 H152 2nd wife of H. Freeman
Matthews Sarah H. d. 5/?/1853 H158 daughter of Joshua & Mary H.
Matthews Louise Freeman b. 6/29/1874 d. 11/16/1966 H177 wife of Harry J., H178

Matthews - McCahey

Matthews   Harry J.   b. 9/22/1875   d. 12/22/1937   H178   husband of Louise F., H177
Matthews   Harrison Belknap   b. 11/28/1904   d. 7/29/1920   H179
Matthews   Joseph   b. 11/20/1804   d. 8/30/1892   H180
Matthews   Edmund L.   d. 9/6/1849   H181   age 2 y. 10 m. 6 d.
Matthews   Elizabeth W.   d. 5/9/1849   H182   age 32
Matthews   Cassandra   d. 3/22/1849   H183   age 8 y. 4 m. 11 d.
Matthews   W. B.   d. 1844   H184
Matthews   Cassandra   d. 1839   H185
Matthews   M. H.   H186
Matthews   Joshua   d. 10/27/1872   H187   age 87
Matthews   Elizabeth M.   b. 3/21/1811   d. 2/25/1883   H188
Matthews   Joshua   H189   listed as H187 in 1931 book
Matthews   Bertha Freeman   b. 8/4/1864   d. 7/30/1940   H206
Matthews   Henry C.   b. 10/4/1844   d. 12/6/1916   H207   husband. of Minnie, H208
Matthews   Minnie   b. 4/12/1853   d. 12/23/1887   H208   wife of Henry C., H207
Matthews   Elizabeth Luke   b. 6/28/1900   d. 10/26/1955   H209   1st wife of H. Freeman, H210
Matthews   H. Freeman   b. 5/26/1899   d. 10/19/1986   H210
Matthews   Sarah H.   d. 5/19/1867   H211   age 87 y. 1 m. 19 d.
Matthews   Thomas   d. 10/1/1864   H212   age 81 y. 9 m.
Matthews   Ann   d. 4/7/1822   H215   age 72
Matthews   Susan R.   H519   no stone
Matthews   Abraham R.   d. 7/11/1893   H520   age 53, no stone
Matthews   Jesse   d. 7/30/1910   H529   age 63, no stone
Matthews   John W.   H530   no stone
Matthews   Mary M.   H532   no stone
Matthews   Aquila Joel   b. 10/27/1871   d. 2/18/1957   J21
Matthews   Lydia Norris   b. 8/11/1872   d. 3/11/1970   J22   daughter of William P. Norris & E. Wilson
McCahey   Elizabeth   d. 2/16/1881   C66
McCahey   John   d. 12/26/1883   C67   age 79

McCahey - Metcalf

McCahey   James   d. 2/10/1882   C68   age 79
McCahey   Rachel   d. 3/22/1885   C69   age 68
McCohan   Howard C.   b. 6/1/1877   d. 1/8/1880   G3   relative to Hattie Cowman
McComas   Susan   d. 6/23/1833   G83
McGuiness   Amy   d. 6/19/1931   I123   age 55, no stone
McKim   John   H285   stone reads J.M.K.
McKim   Mary   d. 1828   H286   no stone
McN. E.   651
McPherson   Edgar J.   b. 7/3/1850   d. 10/31/1897   A188
McPherson   Keith   d. 1940   A188
McPherson   Katherine T.   d. 7/27/1940   A188   age 84
McPherson   Jane   b. 1790   d. 6/12/1876   B41
McPherson   Samuel   d. 12/21/1873   B44   age 75, husband of Ruth A., B44
McPherson   Ruth Anna   d. 10/21/1881   B44   age 67, wife of Samuel
McPherson   Sarah   b. 12/20/1809   d. 3/7/1889   G27E   (G25E) daughter of Isaac & Tacy Ellicott
McPherson   Hannah   b. 4/22/1805   d. 9/29/1893   G28E   (G26E)
Meade   Belle Lowe   A63   bought but not used? 1931 book
Meade   Murrill H.   A64   bought but not used? 1931 book
Medcalf   Isabella   G47
Meijer   Jacob H.   b. 1891   d. 6/?/1926   I493   age 35
Meijer   Elizabeth T.   b. 1891   d. 1963   I493
Mercer   Perry (Percy) G.   b. 10/16/1798   d. 7/18/1884   B38
Mercer   Sarah   b. 9/7/1810   d. 7/5/1879   B39   possibly B37
Meredith   Mary E. Moyer   b. 6/13/1876   d. 9/8/1947   A210
Meredith   Clyde Rabe   d. 8/25/1960   A211   age 89, no stone
Merryman   Eugene   b. 3/31/1872   d. 7/1/1952   C7
Merryman   Ella Corse   b. 11/30/1877   d. 10/31/1966   C8
Merryman   Stephen   C8   buried in this plot
Merryman   Rodherick (Rhodrick)   b. 1/6/1953   d. 1/15/1953   K19
Merryman   Stephen W.   b. 1946   d. 5/9/1962   K20
Metcalf   Isabella   G47   no stone

Meyer - Mullikin

Meyer   Oscar C. Jr.   I393
Meyer   Elizabeth   I394   or possible I392   space saved in 1931 book
Middleton   Mary Probst   d. 2/10/1931   E7   age 48
Miller   Albert   d. 7/5/1886   G22   age 6 w., no stone
Mills   Sarah   d. 4/24/1850   I148   age 40
Mills   Rachael   d. 1849   I212   age 64
Mistretta   Michael Peter?   b. 1900   d. 1978   A277
Mitchell   Joseph B.   b. 9/22/1878   d. 5/22/1941   A87
Mitchell   Gladys B.   b. 2/3/1879   d. 8/26/1927   A88
Mitchell   John   b. 1736   d. 1821   I500
Mitchell   Clara Frazer Martenet   b. 12/2/1890   d. 12/5/1946   J9
Mitchison   Caroline R.   b. 1892   d. 1978   C70   shown on map as C88
Mitchison   Caroline   C88   no stone possibly C70
Mitchison   Gordon B. (A.)   b. 1917   d. 8/16/1932   F13   age 14, nephew of Bertha R.
Mitchison   Bertha R.   b. 1865   d. 3/24/1944   F13   aunt of Gordon R.
Mitchison   William J.   b. 1853   d. 10/27/1926   F14
Moore   James Edward?   d. 7/22/1906?   G68   no stone; possibly M.I. (E.) in 1906 minutes, possibly I70
Moore   Anna Belle   b. 10/1/1863   d. 9/12/1886   H467   daughter of Dr. John F. & Mary, no stone
Moore   James   I70   no stone
Moore   Esther Sinclair   d. 1/3/1891   I69   age 33   no stone
Morgan   Sophia S.   d. 3/10/1882   I319   age 41
Morrow   Miles Webster Sr.   b. 1/27/1920   d. 7/13/1988   A221 "Builder"
Mortland   (Morthland) (Northland) S.   d. 1846   H282
Mott   Gulielma   H533   from 10a book
Mott   two children   H534   no stone
Mott   R. C.   b. 11/3/1791   d. 1/?/1846   H535
Mott   Rachel M.   d. 1863   H536   age 75
Mullikin   Helen Holt   b. 8/12/1871   d. 7/8/1936   I409   wife of Cecil, I410
Mullikin   Cecil   b. 12/29/1866   d. 5/1/1930   I410   husband of Helen, I409

Murry Samuel H531 from 10a book

Narcarrow John I458
Neal E. M. d. 1817 639 age 70
Neall Rebecca B. b. 4/17/1788 d. 11/15/1880 H170
Needles Sarah b. 5/19/1831 d. 12/19/1903 B43
Needles E. Harry (Henry) d. 1837 H137
Needles Elizabeth d. 1833 H139
Needles Susuanah d. 1839 H140
Needles Augusta S. b. 4/16/1837 d. 3/17/1898 H164
Needles John Amos b. 10/1/1828 d. 10/3/1899 H164
Needles Rachel H. d. 3/12/1884 H165 age 86
Needles Edward d. 1/11/1873 H166 age 77
Needles Elizabeth d. 8/30/1870 H169 age 80
Needles Lydia d. 1818 H171
Needles John b. 1786 d. 7/18/1878 H172 age 92
Needles Eliza d. 1840 H173
Needles Caroline d. 1858 H174
Needles Laura d. 1858 H174
Needles Walter M. d. 1/24/1869 H175
Needles Elizabeth d. 12/26/1871 H176 age 6 y. 4 m., daughter. of John L. & ? S.
Newman Emma Bromwell b. 1/15/1870 d. 3/18/1945 J52
Newman Herman b. 10/29/1874 d. 12/10/1945 J52
Norris William T. d. 3/7/1912 age 54, removed to Spring Hill Cemetery, Easton, Maryland
Norris O. C. d. 2/20/1838 600 age 32
Norris George D. d. 9/12/1870 B103 age 6
Norris Sarah L. b. 9/3/1850 d. 8/4/1936 B105
Norris Benjamin F. d. 11/7/1867 B107 age 59
Norris Ann d. 1841 I324 age 70

Norris - Osborn

Norris John Cowman d. 8/18/1917 J23 age 48
Norris Mary Annie b. 2/5/1849 d. 8/22/1933 J24
Norris William Penn b. 1/27/1843 d. 1/6/1913 J25
Noyes Grace Annie Markley b. 12/22/1877 d. 11/27/1973 I87

O

Offley E33 from 10a book
Offley Ella d. 8/19/1871 E34 2 m. 19 d. last name not on stone from 1931 book
Offley Sarah V. d. 8/10/1881 E36 age 78, "mother"
Offley Joseph W. d. 10/30/1889 E37 age 62, "father"
Offley Lydia E. b. 10/25/1844 d. 12/6/1932 E41
Offley Martha Milton b. 10/28/1852 d. 1/13/1923 E42
Offley Annie Edmondson b. 8/28/1848 d. 1/28/1919 E43
Offley Margaret b. 12/2/1856 d. 11/7/1917 E44
Offley Martha Edmondson d. 5/30/1898 E45 age 80, wife of Michael, E46
Offley Michael d. 2/18/1870 E46 age 51, husband of Martha E., E45
Offley Wilson Dennis b. 11/24/1886 d. 7/30/1887 F118 son of Michael & Mary, F120/F121
Offley Norman Griseom? b. 10/5/1882 d. 9/4/1887 F119 son of Michael & Mary, F120/F121
Offley Michael b. 7/19/1816 d. 10/7/1909 F120 husband of Mary G., F121
Offley Mary Griscam b. 6/13/1845 d. 7/15/1925 F121 wife of Michael, F120
Offley Arthur Edward d. 4/26/1888 I360 age 2 y. 6 m., son of Joseph & Alice Elsworth, no stone
Ogden Mary I. d. 1/11/1946 E217 age 89, no stone, listed in 1931 book as M. G. (Gray plot)
Ogunrinde Godwin Akin b. 7/4/1943 d. 1/20/1975 A243
Osborn Mary Cardean Davis b. 4/2/1887 d. 3/7/1969 F97

Owens Willie A.   H504   unreadable stone

P

P. A.   d. 1835   634
Painter   Edward   d. 9/29/1875   E156   age 63
Painter   Louisa Gilpin   d. 5/16/1896   E157   age 81
Painter   Joseph G.   d. 9/12/1878   E158   age 32, moved from E161
Pais   Eliza R.   d. 11/17/1861   H65   age 50, wife of Mahlon
Palmer   A.. Mitchell Jr.   b. 7/22/1903   d. 8/10/1903   A162
Pancoast   Adelaide B.   d. 7/17/1990   J31
Pancoast   Omar Burton Jr.   d. 11/9/1988   J32
Pancoast   Joe? Anne Ross   b. 1874   d. 7/21/1967   J33
Pancoast   Dr. Omar Burton   b. 1871   d. 7/2/1928   J34
Pancost   John   b. 2/23/1771   d. 7/3/1850   B93
Pancost   Susan   b. 11/13/1811   d. 3/14/1893   B94
Pardoe   Eleanor E.   b. 1847   d. 12/4/1917   C56   listed on map as Ellen and in 1931 book as Farbor in 10a book as Tarboe
Parker   John Hollowell   b. 10/9/1891   d. 3/10/1968   C54
Parker   Ruth Pardoe Hunter   b. 1/11/1896   d. 11/18/1981   C55
Parker   Ann   b. 11/17/1865   d. 7/7/1899   G24E
Payne   Mina H.   d. 11/8/1894   B147   age 16 m., grandson of John G. Cowman, no stone
Payne   infant   d. 2/19/1899   B147   age 6 h., child of J.W.M & Alice C., grandchild of J.G. Cowman   from permit & minutes in plot H255
Peacock   L. Lawrence   b. 1904   d. 8/4/1989   F19
Peacock   Esther Hunt   b. 1906   F19
Peck   John S.   d. 4/14/1818   H195   age 45
Penrose   Rhoda Archer   b. 4/5/1876   d. 5/25/1975   E183   wife of William, E184
Penrose   William   b. 6/16/1862   d. 8/24/1937   E184   husband of Rhoda A., E183
Penrose   Susan R.   d. 8/5/1910   E187   age 82, wife of Eliakim G., E188

Penrose - Pope

Penrose Eliakim G. d. 2/12/1882 E188 age 65, husband of Susan R., E187

Penrose Elizabeth (Lizzie) b. 10/5/1860 d. 2/5/1866 E189 daughter of Eliakim C. & Susan R., E187/E188

Perkins Lucretia D. d. 3/11/1868 E35 age 68

Pine Mary H. d. 10/15/1868 E138 age 73 y. 9 m. 22 d., from New Jersey

Pine Joshua S. d. 11/5/1878 E139 age 87 y. 9 m. 21 d, from New Jersey

Plummer Richard b. 12/25/1862 d. 5/6/1871 H15 son of I. & F.P., possible last name Lancaster from 1931 book

Plummer Elizabeth Byrnes b. 3/6/1867 d. 7/30/1867 H16 daughter. of F.W. & E.B., H17/H18

Plummer Elizabeth Byrnes b. 10/26/1839 d. 7/1/1872 H17 wife of Francis W., H18

Plummer Francis W. b. 7/9/1849 d. 10/12/1904 H18 husband of Elizabeth B., H17

Plummer Philip S. b 9/6/1876 d. 5/10/1938 H19 possible last name Goulding

Plummer Richard d. 8/12/1870 H25 age 65

Plummer Elizabeth G. d. 2/17/1838 H26 age 29

Plummer Ruth Byrnes d. 6/11/1850 H27 age 56

Plummer Joanna b. 2/22/1818 d. 11/25/1883 H28

Plummer Henrietta d. 12/13/1862 H29 age 76

Plummer Rebecca b. 10/16/1812 d. 2/20/1884 H30

Plummer Richard d. 10/10/1852 I74 age 2 w., buried with Sarah Corkran

Pollard Seth I183 no stone

Pope Franklyn Chandlee d. 7/24/1885 F69 age 7 m., son of W.R. & Rebecca

Pope Elizabeth Ann d. 7/26/1932 F72 age 82, no stone

Pope Franklin F. b. 1/1/1809 d. 4/27/1893 F73

Pope Mary E. b. 3/19/1819 d. 11/3/1882 F74

Pope Ann d. 8/15/1870 H502 age 83

Pope Folger d. 3/12/1855 H503 age 75

Pope - Poultney

Pope   Dorothy   b. 10/2/1888   d. 3/13/1977   I163   plot is listed on map in 2 places; one at end of the row has no stone

Pope   Rosina Upshire   b. 4/9/1856   d. 8/2/1942   I164   wife of George B., I165

Pope   George Bayard   b. 5/9/1858   d. 6/30/1893   I165   husband of Rosina U., I164

Pope   Bayard   b. 1883   d. 1884   I166   son of George & Rosina, I164/165

Pope   Guilelma   b. 4/4/1871   d. 5/20/1877   I167

Pope   David Sands   b. 1838   d. 4/29/1921   I171   husband of Sarah R.

Pope   Sarah R.   d. 11/22/1888   I172   age 84, wife of David S.

Pope   David S.   d. 1840   I173   age 14

Pope   Daniel Franklyn   b. 8/20/1833   d. 4/16/1916   I174

Pope   Hannah More   b. 4/23/1840   d. 4/29/1918   I175

Pope   Mary E.   b. 1874   d. 11/4/1955   I176   no stone, possibly I178

Pope   Benjamin F.   b. 1852   d. 10/22/1937   I177

Pope   David Berkham   b. 1872   d. 1/20/1893   I179   Berkam?

Potee   Julia H.   b. 2/?/1827   d. 6/11/1881   G45

Potee   Peter P.   G46

Potter   Sarah Jane   b. 9/10/1828   d. 5/13/1919   H190

Potter   Howard   I142   from 10a book

Potts   Abbie C.   d. 3/31/1871   B111   age 3 y. 3 w.

Potts   Edith A.   d. 3/31/1871   B112   age 19 m..

Potts   Aagot   b. 8/22/1899   d. 4/14/1986   B113

Potts   Norman N.   b. 4/31/1912   d. 5/13/1980   B114

Potts   Mary Compton   b. 11/22/1879   d. 9/2/1962   B115

Potts   Norman Newport Sr.   b. 11/25/1875   d. 2/1/1940   B116

Poultney   Jane T. E.   d. 2/24/1887   F27   wife of Thomas, F28

Poultney   Thomas P. Jr.   d. 1834   F28   husband of Jane, F27

Poultney   Eliza   d. 1849   F30

Poultney   Benjamin   b. 9/18/1815   d. 8/15/1872   F31

Poultney   Phillip   b. 5/18/1799   d. 8/10/1869   F34

Poultney   Ann R.   d. 7/?/1885   F66   age 34

Poultney   Elizabeth   d. 1/22/1855   I79   age 69

Powell - Procter

Powell Henry J. b. 3/20/1803 d. 3/19/1888 H397 from Hyde Park, New York
Powell Louisa J. b. 8/1/1832 d. 11/27/1884 H398 born Chatham, New York
Powell Margaret d. 6/4/1861 I381 age 86
Price Benjamin b. 11/21/1844 d. 4/2/1909 B27
Price Mary M. b. 8/19/1852 d. 4/20/1910 B28 Walker? from 10a book
Price Adelaide C. b. 1885 d. 1960 B29
Price Russell Richardson b. 4/27/1887 d. 4/10/1972 B31 son of Benjamin Price & Mary Linhard
Price 2 children B32 of Benjamin, no stone
Price Ann M. d. 1855 H474
Price H. d. 1854 H476
Price Emily W. b. 3/12/1853 d. 12/29/1887 I17 daughter of Joshua & Phoebe
Price Elizabeth M. b. 1818 d. 1874 I18 "Lizzie"
Price Thomas b. 3/24/1858 d. 4/24/1868 I21
Price Sarah Jane d. 8/6/1901 I255
Probst Emilie Wood b. 7/30/1895 d. 1/9/1980 Section E, memorial stone above E8
Probst Carrie Mae b. 2/13/1882 d. 6/28/1975 Section E, memorial stone above E7
Probst Emile Wood b. 6/30/1856 d. 4/28/1944 E8
Probst Rev. Luther Kolb d. 2/1/1920 E9 age 63, grandson of William Wood
Probst Luther Kolb Jr. b. 7/30/1895 d. 1/28/1907 E10
Probst Lillian d. 9/12/1891 E11 age 5 m. 17 d., granddaughter of William Wood
Probst William Wood d. 4/30/1889 E12 age 2 y. 4 m. 2 d., "Willie"
Probst child E13 no stone
Procter Edward d. 1846 H418 age 30
Procter Rebecca d. 8/7/1863 H419 age 38
Procter William d. 1/15/1860 H420 age 80
Procter Anna (Ann) d. 1/26/1861 H421 age 71

Procter   Deborah W.   b. 10/22/1870   d. 2/17/1898   H422
Pugh   Ann P.   b. 10/10/1865   H194   age 82
Pugh   Elizabeth   d. 1843   I190   age 70
Pusey   Nathan   d. 5/21/1865   H376   age 75
Pusey   Mary M.   d. 7/29/1874   H377   age 73
Pusey   John Marsh   H416

R.   E. & H.   H450
Ramsey   Francis A.   b. 5/22/1822   d. 2/25/1890   G9
Ramsey   Joseph E.   b. 8/21/1816   d. 12/14/1880   G10
Ramsey   Sadie F.   b. 5/23/1872   d. 9/15/1875   G11
Read   Caroline   1/14/1894   E4   age 75; date on stone probably death
Read   Martha Jane   d. 12/19/1922   I184   age 77
Read   Larken   b. 1810   d. 4/5/1893   I184   age 82
Read   Ellen   (Nellie)   d. 1887   I185
Read   child   I186   of Oliver, no stone
Read   Grace B.   d. 1/16/1869   I188   age 68
Read   Amos   d. 3/29/1848   I189   age 62
Read   Oliver C.   b. 9/?/1798   d. 2/?/1835   I263   husband of Francis V., I264
Read   Frances Virginia   b. 5/10/1842   d. 9/13/1908   I264   wife of Oliver C., I263
Read   Adella B.   b. 11/10/1874   d. 1/26/1909   I265
Read   Maud W.   b. 5/19/1877   d. 4/11/1915   I266
Read   Charles A.   b. 5/18/1863   d. 3/28/1931   I267
Read   William H.   b. 1832   d. 10/28 1920   J4   "father"
Read   Julia A.   b. 1838   d. 10/28/1920   J5   "mother"
Read   Oliver Ellsworth   b. 8/20/1861   d. 11/13/1936   J16   "brother"
Read   Alice Gertrude   b. 9/23/1871   d. 9/13/1937   J17   "sister"
Read   Erla (Enola) Ida   b. 10/13/1879   d. 3/3/1962   J18   "sister"

Read - Reese

Read   L. Frank   b. 8/6/1869   d. 7/11/1947   J19   "father"
Read   Lydia Belle   b. 1/11/1872   d. 8/8/1918   J20   "mother"
Reed   John O. Cornthwaite   d. 2/27/1898   Section J from 98 minutes and 9b book from #14 book Oliver E. Plot J?
Reese   Harry Stabler   d. 3/2/1924   from permit & minutes disenterred and placed in Druid Ridge Cemetery (9b)
Reese   Martha Stabler   d. 10/15/1911   B5   age 86
Reese   Thomas M.   d. 7/31/1909   B6   age 90
Reese   Mary T.   d. 6/18/1929   B7   age 69, wife of Lawrence M. Reese
Reese   Walter   d. 4/22/1880   B8   age 28
Reese   Frank   b. 11/21/1847   d. 4/16/1865   B9
Reese   Edward   d. 5/8/1895   B61   age 70
Reese   Mary A.   d. 6/30/1906   B62   age 72
Reese   Katherine S.   d. 3/3/1926   B63   age 68, daughter of Edward & Mary A., B61/B62
Reese   Francis Gilpin   d. 5/18/1928   B64   age 72
Reese   James Stone   b. 4/11/1862   d. 4/1/1913   B65   husband of Alice, B66, son of Edward & Mary A. (Gilpin) Reese, B61/B62
Reese   Alice   d. 5/12/1918   B66   age 68, wife of James S., B65
Reese   Edward Bartlett   b. 12/18/1890   d. 4/19/1943   B67   cremation
Reese   Beatrice F. Heath   b. 12/1/1902   d. 5/23/1982   B68
Reese   Mary E.   d. 6/27/1943   C110   age 85 y. 2 m. 10 d., no stone
Reese   Mabel Meredith   b. 1/28/1876   d. 1/10/1969   F6   daughter of Henry Reese & ? Miller, on burial certificate as F2
Reese   Caroline Miller   b. 5/10/1868   d. 3/18/1947   F7
Reese   Anne Lacy   b. 2/15/1865   d. 2/2/1945   F8
Reese   Maryanna A.   b 3/4/1838   d. 3/20/1931   F9
Reese   Henry   b. 5/21/1830   d. 3/13/1910   F10
Reese   Deborah   b. 6/26/1827   d. 1/6/1910   F11
Reese   Arthur Lacy   b. 10/30/1867   d. 3/12/1894   F12
Reese   Cornelia S.   b. 4/1/1860   d. 1/13/1946   H75
Reese   Elizabeth Moore   b. 10/23/1818   d. 1/28/1902   H76
Reese   Sarah Jane   b. 10/3/1820   d. 12/1/1906   H77
Reese   Gerard H.   b. 9/8/1818   d. 8/31/1879   H78

Reese Thomas L.   b. 6/28/1846   d. 12/7/1890   H79
Reese Mary M.   b. 1788   d. 1872   H80
Reese Thomas L.   d. 4/11/1863   H81
Reese Mary Ann   b. 1853   d. 1855   H82
Regester E. (Elizabeth)   I119   no stone
Regester Samuel (Sam)   I120   no stone
Regester Amanda   d. 9/14/1913   I181   age 83
Regester John   d. 12/27/1896   I182   age 73, buried with Eliza Weigel, unreadable stone
Reigart Sarah C.   d. 1/28/1889   F46   age 63
Resh Mary Louise B.   b. 6/22/1906   d. 9/21/1936   F1
Resh Grace   F2   no stone
Rice Mary E.   F112
Richards Florence M. Chamberlain   b. 1/16/1897   d. 8/4/1978   A110
Richards Charles Randolph   b. 6/10/1889   d. 4/3/1965   A111
Richards Susan K. (C.)   b. 2/8/1851   d. 10/14/1922   A112
Richards Randolph J.   b. 7/25/1853   d. 4/14/1928   A113
Richards Edward   b. 4/7/1822   d. 9/15/1899   C43   husband of Rebecca B., C47
Richards Nicholas G.   b. 8/2/1851   d. 1/10/1908   C44   son of Edward & Rebecca B., C43/C47
Richards Eleanora (Ella) V.   b. 11/21/1856   d. 12/4/1934   C45
Richards Anna S.   b. 1/31/1859   d. 11/30/1930   C46   from 10a book   A146
Richards Rebecca B.   b. 7/24/1829   d. 5/17/1905   C47   wife of Edward, C43
Richards William Henry   d. 4/23/1897   C48   age 25, son of Edward & Rebecca B., C43/C47
Richards twin sons   C48   of Edward, C43
Richardson Sarah   G61   no stone
Riley Clara S.   d. 1811   F47   age 26
Riley Dr. William   d. 8/15/1887   F48   age 80
Riley E. Ellen   d. 5/6/1876   F49   age 56
Riley William   d. 8/25/1825   F50

Riley - Russ

Riley Sarah d. 1819 F51 age 82
Riley Valerius d. 7/18/1866 H505 age 76
Riley Catherine E. d. 5/24/1890 H510 age 77
Riley Samuel S. d. 11/29/1877 H511 age 69
Roberts Elizabeth d. 1812 H111
Roberts Mary F. b. 6/30/1852 d. 11/7/1890 H566
Roberts Lydia F. b. 8/3/1824 d. 4/20/1894 H567 wife of Josiah, H568
Roberts Josiah b. 3/26/1823 d. 7/4/1901 H568 husband of Lydia, H567
Roberts Isabel Chambers b. 11/30/1869 d. 1/13/1964 K2
Roberts Robert French b. 8/19/1862 d. 5/14/1940 K3
Roberts Ellen T. b. 9/14/1854 d. 2/20/1922 K5
Roberts Caroline b. 9/30/1807 d. 11/29/1866 H366
Robertson E. d. 1832 642
Robinson Camilla d. 10/9/1911 B 24 age 66
Robinson Deborah b. 9/30/1807 d. 11/29/1866 H366
Robinson William b. 1865 H368 age 60
Rogers Henry A. d. 1/12/1836 632
Roloson Francis S. b. 11/20/1842 d. 7/30/1927 I9
Roloson wife of Francis I9½ unmarked, from 3x5 card
Roloson Richard H. d. 12/23/1913 I10 age 75
Roloson wife of Richard I10½ unmarked, from 3x5 card
Roloson Albert S. d. 8/27/1895 I10½ age 1 d., possibly I9½
Roloson Hugh b. 4/20/1806 d. 11/12/1883 I12
Roloson Eliza b. 10/5/1805 d. 11/27/1880 I13
Roloson Albert S. b. 2/7/1879 d. 4/23/1962 I49
Roloson Cora E. b. 1/10/1871 d. 2/4/1956 I50
Roloson Gerterude Mary b. 2/14/1877 d. 6/17/1958 I51
Ross Lydia Gover Hull d. 11/8/1906 F86 age 32, daughter of William & Carrie R. Hull, F86/F87, unreadable stone
Ross Sarah Linton b. 1836 d. 4/24/1927 J35
Roumach Christina b. 9/12/1823 d. 1/15/1913 E1
Russ Seymour William d. 4/1 1920 I365 age 4 d., no stone

Russell   Gertrude Sullivan   b. 1873   d. 5/19/1959   A230
Russell   Dr. Henry   b. 1873   d. 12/2/1950   A231
Russell   John   d. 5/9/1890   B69   age 69, husband of Mary H., B70
Russell   Mary H.   b. 11/11/1890   d. 12/29/1916   B70   wife of John Russell, B69
Russell   John T.   d. 7/11/1893   B71?   age 53, listed as family plot on permit
Russell   Annie Kemp   d. 2/23/1919   B73
Russell   Charles   d. 6/10/1919   d. B73½   age 78
Russell   Mary Bailey   b. 7/23/1813   d. 3/18/1893   B74   wife of Thomas, B75
Russell   Thomas   b. 12/31/1810   d. 1/9/1878   B75   husband of Mary B., B74
Russell   Ida Richards   b. 1864   d. 2/15/1940   C42
Russell   John S.   b. 1869   d. 5/13/1940   C42
Russell   Jesse   b. 3/5/1810   d. 10/17/1892   G31

S

S. H.   615
S. R.   d. 1823   660
S. M.   1523
Sanderson   Ross   A269   no stone, possibly A270
Sanderson   Ross Warren   b. 2/20/1884   d. 9/26/1983   A270
Sanderson   Lucille Harris   b. 5/28/1884   d. 4/7/1962   A270
Sanks   George W.   d. 5/4/1887   age 60, from minutes
Satterthwaite   Ellen G.   d. 9/12/1899   H448   age 93, no stone
Saul   Joseph W.   d. 2/20/1900   H449   age 86, husband of Ann, H494, no stone
Saul   Ann   H494   no stone, wife of Saul, H449
Saunders   Ida O. Schorreck   b. 7/9/1884   d. 3/4/1953   A245
Scharff   Isaac   b. 11/?/1808   d. 3/?/1879   I117
Scharff   Mary A.   b. 4/?/1809   d. 5/?/1875   I118

Schloss - Sheppard

Schloss   Elizabeth   d. 1914   F18
Schofield   Joseph   b. 1813   d. 6/23/1889   B11   by his son
Schooley   Ella B.   d. 7/9/1937   C89   age 78, no stone
Schooley   Florence W.   d. 1/6/1927   C91   age 79
Schooley   Elmer J.   d. 11/22/1911   C92   age 45
Schooley   John William   d. 12/6/1911   C93
Schooley   Effie Ann   d. 11/25/1942   C94   age 80 y. 2 m., not on stone
Schooley   Elizabeth D.   d. 11/11/1906   C94   age 55
Schooley   Estelle M.   d. 1905   C95   age 46, given in memory by the children of St. Peters School
Schooley   Hannah   b. 10/30/1825   d. 4/25/1912   C96
Schooley   William H.   d. 8/5/1892   C97   age 82
Scott   Rossiter   d. 1830   665
Scott   Edith   d. 1832   666
Scott   Jeffery Forbush   b. 4/26/1951   d. 5/10/1951   A238
Scott   Mary Amelia   b. 12/7/1880   d. 10/3/1956   A241
Scott   Harry Shane Sr.   b. 7/12/1877   d. 9/4/1943   A242
Scott   James   G23   no stone
Scudder   Sophia G.   d. 2/2/1918   G13   age 65, no stone
Scudder   Rachel M.   b. 8/10/1820   d. 6/23/1876   G14
Sears   Ann Maria   b. 9/13/1826   d. 7/2/1919   B87   daughter of Ward & Anna Sears
Sears   Hannah W.   d. 1839   I36
Sewell   Susan   d. 2/16/1894   H447   age 85, no stone
Sharp   Alpheus P.   d. 10/10/1909   H246   age 85
Sharp   Anna Matthews   d. 3/7/1894   H247   age 66
Sharp   George Matthews   d. 7/7/1911   H248   age 59
Sharples   Esther Foulks   b. 1878   d. 10/2/1958   A219
Sharples   Henry R.   b. 1874   d. 1963   A219
Shaw   Morris   b. 1/29/1810   d. 10/18/1842   H83
Shedd   Jepthar   d. 1833   I308
Shellman   infant   b. 6/11/1924   d. 6/11/1924   A116   child of Mary Winslow Shellman, grandchild of Dr. Randolph Winslow
Sheppard   Rebecca W.   670

Sheppard- Sipe

Sheppard   Nathan   d. 11/21/1834   671
Sherwood   Albert Bartlett   b. 5/5/1886   d. 10/21/1890   H104
Shield   M. K.   669
Shield   Sarah B.   d. 3/13/1863   I38
Shield   Rachel   d. 7/21/1857   I39   age 91
Shields   Susan M.   G49   no stone
Shinn   Laura Barber   b. 1880   d. 9/14/1957   A158   inscription on stone A.N.C.,B.H.41,A.E.F.
Shipley   Elmer A.   d. 5/16/1944   E110   age 74, no stone
Shipley   Molly   b. 9/7/1888   d. 8/10/1889   E113   no stone
Shipley   Grace   d. 6/1/1890   E114   age 4 m., no stone
Shipley   George Wesley   d. 5/3/1892   E115   age 1 m., no stone
Shipley   W. Hamnond   d. 12/2/1893   E116   age 6 m., no stone
Shipley   Bertie E.   d. 11/18/1886   E117   age 7 m., stone in site has name Carrie Shipley, unreadable otherwise
Shipley   Carrie   E118   unreadable stone
Shipley   Mary Alice   b. 10/1/1856   d. 8/10/1933   E122 1/2   "mother"
Shipley   William H.   b. 5/23/1843   d. 3/2/1923   E123   "father"
Shoemaker   child   I1   no stone
Shoemaker   Martha A.   d. 8/21/1902   I4   age 65
Shoemaker   George   d. 9/28/1890   I5   age 65
Shoemaker   Jonathan S.   b. 5/25/1817   d. 12/7/1867   I6
Shoemaker   Alfred   b. 12/26/1818   d. 3/12/1866   I7
Shoemaker   Charles   b. 11/17/1788   d. 4/9/1847   I225
Shoemaker   Francis Hartley   b. 1867   d. 10/15/1928   I32
Shropshire   William B.   d. 4/21/1836   630
Sidwell   Mary Milner   b. 2/14/1794   d. 3/11/1867   F37
Sinclair   Esther   d. 2/30/1853   I129
Sinclair   Robert   d. 10/27/1853   I130   age 81
Sipe   Carolyn Carter   b. 3/10/1911   d. 12/19/1985   A175   wife of Samuel F., A176
Sipe   Samuel F.   b. 2/20/1917   d. 1/10/1993   A176   husband of Carolyn C., A175

Sipe - Stabler

Smith   Mary Alice   b. 2/7/1866   d. 5/4/1936   C48a   wife of Samuel, C48b
Smith   Samuel   b. 4/19/1864   d. 3/25/1947   C48b   husband of Mary A., C48a
Smith   William   d. 12/25/1888   G27   age 72, no stone
Smith   Betsy   b. 5/9/1810   d. 7/30/1870   G28
Smith   Samuel B.   b. 3/3/1806   d. 5/27/1876   I170
Smith   Matthew M.   d. 1834   I236   in 1931 book as Nathan
Smith   Mary   J11   no stone
Smith   Mary Wheeler   d. 12/4/1920   J14   age 66
Smith   Theodore (Theodric)   d. 3/21/1931   J15   age 86
Smothers   Bealah   G18   no stone, name from 10a book Smithers
Snodgrass   Hannah C.   b. 12/27/1813   d. 6/8/1889   F75   age 76, daughter of Benjamin C. & Elizabeth Matthews
Snowden   Sarah   d. 5/8/1871   B124   age 66
Southcomb   Theodore Pope   d. 8/6/1902   G96   age 77, unreadable stone
Southcomb   Peter Henry   d. 6/20/1888   G95   age 65, son of Carey & Alicianna Ford, unreadable stone
Southcomb   Lydia Lovegrove   b. 1865   d. 12/22/1969   G97
Southcomb   Alice   b. 1859   d. 11/1/1950   G97
Southcomb   Mary Read   d. 10/23/1951   G98   age 90, no stone listed on G97 stone
Spencer   Eloiza D.   b. 7/29/1814   d. 2/2/1894   C109
Spencer   William Lewis   b. 10/4/1865   d. 4/1/1937   C112   "Willie"
Spencer   Elizabeth J.   b. 12/24/1860   d. 12/31/1935   C113
Spencer   Sarah Elizabeth   d. 7/2/1917   C114   age 76, wife of John M., C115
Spencer   John M.   d. 11/28/1881   C115   age 65, husband of Sarah E., C114
Spencer   Elizabeth   d. 1838   H135
Stabler   Edward Albert   b. 9/11/1878   d. 12/14/1958   E88
Stabler   Helen   b. 4/25/1871   d. 1/13/1876   E89
Stabler   Louise   b. 5/17/1828   d. 10/15/1870   E90
Stabler   Eliza Butler   b. 2/16/1841   d. 5/6/1918   E91

Stabler   Edward Jr.   b. 3/16/1836   d. 6/3/1923   E92
Stabler   Corrine M. (A.)   b. 11/10/1885   d. 10/25/1956   E93
Stabler   Clinton   b. 11/19/1859   d. 7/7/1860   H56   son of Francis
Stabler   Lydia C.   b. 12/22/1834   d. 5/23/1883   H264   granddaughter of Lydia Jeffries, H265
Stansbury   Susanna   d. 7/29/1853   675   age 22
Starr   William Penn   d. 1/22/1866   age 4 y. 27 d., "Willie "
Starr   Mary E.   b. 12/17/1863   d. 2/28/1955   H477a   or H476
Starr   Benjamin Frank   d. 1/26/1882   H478   age 63
Starr   Mary E.   d. 11/18/1894   H479   age 72
Starr   George Amoss   d. 9/4/1895   H480   age 36
Starr   William Thomas   d. 2/1/1921   H482   age 65
Starr   Sallie Hunt   d. 11/4/1914   H483   age 56
Starr   Benjamin Frank II   b. 9/18/1855   d. 2/2/1915   H484
Starr   Annie D.   b. 8/17/1855   d. 5/25/1933   H485
Starr   M. Elanor   b. 11/26/1882   d. 3/19/1975   H486
Starr   Benjamin Frank III   b. 5/13/1889   d. 1/20/1926   H487
Stearns   Elmira   d. 8/4/1860   B88   age 39, wife of George, B90
Stearns   Albert Carter   b. 6/21/1851   d. 5/21/1911   B89   son of Elmira & George, B88/B90
Stearns   George Henry   b. 11/24/1848   d. 1/17/1919   B90   husband of Elmira, B88
Stewart   Fanny   d. 3/15/1942   E104   age 84, no stone
Stewart   Joseph J.   b. 5/1/1828   d. 1/19/1882   E105   husband of Mary, E106
Stewart   Mary   b. 9/9/1831   d. 8/2/1878   E106   wife of Joseph J., E105
Stewart   Mary   b. 5/27/1858   d. 7/8/1868   E107   daughter of Joseph J. & Mary, E105/106
Stewart   Mary   d. 1836   I475   age 15 m. 21 d.
Stewart   Caroline   d. 1834   I494
Storke   Richard W.   d. 1/29/1867   H198   age 25
Stratton   Samuel W.   d. 1850   659
Stump   George E. (C.)   b. 3/5/1839   d. 3/21/1893   H453
Stump   Susan R.   b. 1849   d. 3/1/1928   H454

Sutton - Taylor

Sutton   Ella   b. 12/20/1852   d. 3/4/1928   H383
Sutton   Lucy   b. 1/10/1848   d. 7/1/1919   H384
Sutton   Cora   H385   unreadable stone
Sutton   James S. (L.)   b. 12/26/1806   d. 12/15/1887   H386
Sutton   Elizabeth M.   d. 12/17/1887   H387   age 60, unsure of date
Sutton   Elizabeth   d. 7/20/1838   H388   age 13 m.
Sutton   Maltier   d. 1855   H389   age 17
Sutton   Ellen   d. 1849   H390   age 2 y. 6 m.
Swain   Louisa A.   d. 4/25/1880   F124   age 79, wife of Stephen, F125
Swain   Stephen   d. 10/6/1872   F125   age 77, husband of Louisa A., F124
Swain   Georgiana   d. 1/22/1889   G62   age 47, daughter of Henry & Heneretta Fisher Frasher
Swann   William F.   G63   no stone
Swayne   Eliza   d. 1851   625
Sweeney   Mary Ann   d. 5/8/1879   I379

T

T.   E.   d. 1826   668
T.   J.   I206   no stone
Tanboe   Ellan E.   d. 12/6/1917   from 1917 minutes
Tarbert   Elizabeth H.   b. 5/28/1862   d. 12/11/1940   H435
Tarbert   Alexander   b. 12/5/1849   d. 10/30/1926   H436
Taylor   N. W.   674
Taylor   Florence K. Mathews   b. 3/12/1865   d. 3/30/1952   E196
Taylor   Thomas Newbold   b. 4/20/1859   d. 6/20/1935   E197
Taylor   L. Emma   d. 6/13/1923   F 94   age 80, unreadable stone from 10a book F93
Taylor   Jonathan K.   b. 9/3/1838   d. 8/6/1916   F96 from 10a book F94
Taylor   Mary G.   b. 6/17/1874   d. 9/21/1947   G37
Taylor   Henry T.   b. 2/28/1832   d. 12/30/1893   H495

Taylor - Thornton

Taylor Susan Bartlett b. 1/28/1834 d. 6/27/1893 H496 map shows 1896
Teller Mary d. 7/20/1896 on permit and 1896 minutes
Terry Abbie A. d. 10/14/1895 H401 age 60, daughter of Charles & Susan von Trump, H402/403
Thomas Elizabeth d. 1837 636
Thomas Grace Walton b. 1911 d. 4/19/1951 H34
Thomas Wilfred L. b. 11/5/1916 d. 1941 H35 age 24
Thomas wife of Richard H. d. 2/28/1976 H36 from letter to L. Peacock dated 12/5/1977
Thomas Richard Henry b. 1876 d. 1/9/1924 H36
Thomas Alfred L. H37 from 1931 book
Thomas Richard Henry Jr. b. 1908 d. 2/14/1913 H37 age 5
Thomas Mildred L. H37 from 3x5 cards, from 10a book Wilfred
Thomas Louise P. b. 1867 d. 11/24/1920 H38 daughter of Richard P. & Harriet, H39/40
Thomas Harriet Cowman b. 1836 d. 12/16/1935 H39 age 98 y. 11 m. 29 d., wife of Richard P., H40
Thomas Richard Pierce b. 1836 d. 1/7/1911 H40 husband of Harriet C., H39
Thomas Mabel b. 6/24/1862 d. 2/26/1865 H41 daughter of Richard & Harriet, H39/40
Thomas Margaret d. 7/16/1861 H42 age 8 m. 16 d.
Thomas Henrietta M. d. 1/17/1874 H313
Thomas Richard H. M.D. b. 6/20/1805 d. 1/15/1860 H314
Thomas Richard H. Jr. b. 1/18/1844 d. 7/4/1853 H315
Thomas Phoebe C. b. 6/29/1818 d. 2/27/1855 H316
Thomas Mary H317
Thomas Martha C. d. 11/20/1856 H318
Thomas Anna Andrews b. 1868 d. 3/22/1950 J39
Thomas Thaddeus P. b. 1867 d. 3/30/1936 J40
Thompson Mary A. d. 9/22/1902 G69 age 56, no stone
Thornberg J. d. 1820 H283
Thornton Fannie Haws H542 from 10a book

Tilden - Troupe

Tilden   Charles W.   b. 10/10/1839   d. 2/13/1844   620
Tiller   Mary M.   d. 7/19/1896   H430   age 83
Tiller   F. W.   d. 8/4/1882   H431   age 72
Timbres   Nancy Anne Janney   b. 8/20/1923   d. 6/20/1927   E23½ daughter of Harry J. & Rebecca S. J. Timbres; granddaughter of Dr. O. E. Janney, E21
Townsend   Mary   d. 5/7/1799   672
Townsend   Martha S.   d. 11/6/1822   H200½   age 84, daughter of Samuel & Jane S. Townsend, H202/H203
Townsend   Mary   d. 1847   H201
Townsend   Samuel   d. 1/18/1883   H202   age 75, husband of Jane S., H203
Townsend   Jane S.   d. 8/30/1868   H203   wife of Samuel, H202
Townsend   Rachel L. Husband   d. 9/22/1920   H239
Townsend   H. F (E.)   H244
Townsend   Esther H.   H245
Townsend   Joseph C.   b. 6/14/1835   d. 7/17/1912   H353   husband of Mary H., H354
Townsend   Mary H.   b. 5/5/1834   d. 10/27/1903   H354   wife of Joseph C., H353
Travers   Emma R.   b. 1/1/1847   d. 4/7/1916   I341
Travers   Mezzick O.   b. 5/14/1816   d. 11/8/1900   I342
Trego   D. S.   d. 1835   643
Trego   I. D.   d. 1835   644   age 27
Trimble   T. B.   d. 1835   645   age 27
Trimble   George W.   d. 10/6/1909   H332   age 86, no stone
Trimble   David B.   d. 3/15/1900   H333   no stone
Trimble   Mary W.   d. 6/12/1890   H334   age 60   no stone
Trimble   Hannah Mary   b. 3/23/1826   d. 2/9/1926   H335½
Trimble   Mary   d. 1836   H337
Troth   William M.   d. 5/8/1852   H122   age 63
Troupe   Stephanie Murphy   b. 12/26/1922   d. 3/30/1992   F79   daughter of Clark Murphy, husband of Baker H. Troupe
Troupe   Raymond Bowen   d. 7/3/1888   F80   age 1, unreadable stone

Troupe	Merrill H. Jr.	F81 possibly buried in this plot
Troupe	Merrill H. Sr.	b. 7/25/1886 d. 12/28/1955 F81
Troupe	Margaret George	b. 7/24/1818 d. 2/6/1951 F82
Troupe	Hattie Hull	b. 10/6/1861 d. 11/19/1923 F83
Troupe	Calvin F.	b. 7/14/1857 d. 12/29/1942 F84
Trump	Susan Howell	b. 10/26/1805 d. 7/27/1862 H402
Trump	Charles	b. 9/17/1807 d. 3/1/1889 H403
Tucker	S. L.	b. 6/20/1800 d. 8/29/1867 G88
Tucker	Elizabeth	b. 3/27/1811 d. 7/13/1861 G89
Tucker	Margaret	G90 no stone
Tudor	Sarah W.	b. 3/23/1831 d. 11/20/1895 B72 shown on map as B71
Turner	Charles Yardley	b. 1850 d. 1/1/1919 H43
Turner	Joseph	b. 2/8/1841 d. 1/9/1909 H44
Turner	J. Ilena Preston	b. 12/12/1836 d. 2/19/1910 H45
Turner	John	d. 10/20/1916 H46 age 77
Turner	John C.	d. 3/11/1877 H46 age 61
Turner	Thomas G.	b. 9/17/1845 d. 1/21/1916 H47 brother of Elizabeth T. Graham & Charles Yardley Turner
Turner	Hannah B.	d. 5/3/1863 H47 age 46, wife of John R.
Turner	Edward J.	d. 7/19/1875 H49 age 28
Turner	Bertha	d. 6/4/1892 H50 age 5, child of Joseph, no stone
Turner	child	H51 of Joseph, no stone.
Turner	Samuel R.	d. 2/20/1927 H53 age 78, no stone
Turner	Rebecca	b. 10/17/1797 d. 1/16/1877 H99
Turner	Joseph	d. 4/21/1859 H100 age 59
Turner	Lucy	d. 3/31/1855 H101 age 1 m., daughter of J.C. & H.B.
Turner	Janette	d. 2/27/1855 H103 age 2 y. 4 m., daughter of J.C. & H.B.
Tuttle	Louisa C.	b. 3/15/1856 d. 8/8/1936 I355
Tuttle	Arthur J.	b. 4/23/1861 d. 9/19/1912 I356 in 9b book as Alfred
Tyson	Mary	d. 1837 603 niece of Nathan, H289
Tyson	Horaria	d. 1836 612
Tyson	Louise	d. 2/11/1837 613
Tyson	Elisha. E..	d. 2/16/1824 614

Tyson - Tyson

Tyson	William	616A
Tyson	Mary S.	b. 3/2/1801 d. 6/19/1887 B125 wife of Thomas
Tyson	Emily B.	d. 2/3/1873 C30 age 35
Tyson	Elizabeth	d. 4/29/1873 C31 age 70
Tyson	Charles B.	b. 10/15/1806 d. 11/15/1884 C32
Tyson	Margaret	H288½ unreadable stone from Aisquith
Tyson	Evan d. 1832 H288½ from Aisquith
Tyson	Mary d. 1826 H289 from Aisquith
Tyson	Nathan d. 1837 H289
Tyson	Charlotte E. d. 1856 d. 11/22/1897 H540
Tyson	Isaac H541 husband of Fannie Thornton, H542, son of Hannah
Tyson	Fannie Haws Thornton b. 7/4/1837 d. 3/13/1891 H542 wife of Isaac Tyson, H541
Tyson	Anna b. 5/10/1804 d. 4/6/1832 H543 wife of Joseph ?
Tyson	Harriett Berry b. 9/2/1883 d. 2/18/1978 H546 buried with James W. Tyson 3rd
Tyson	Jesse H546 from 10a book
Tyson	James Wood 3rd b. 12/2/1883 d. 3/21/1950 H546½
Tyson	infant H547 daughter of M.D. & M.S.T.
Tyson	Elizabeth H. d. 1/24/1888 H548 age 60, wife of James, H549
Tyson	James Wood b. 7/6/1828 d. 12/3/1900 H549 husband of Elizabeth, H548, son of Hannah & Isaac Jr.
Tyson	Mordecai Dawson b. 1/16/1855 d. 6/6/1901 H550
Tyson	Margaret Sprigg b. 3/2/1859 d. 1/5/1945 H550A
Tyson	Isaac b. 6/6/1859 d. 4/30/1908 H551
Tyson	Jesse b. 7/22/1820 d. 11/28/1906 H552
Tyson	Hannah Ann b. 11/24/1797 d. 1/9/1866 H553
Tyson	Isaac Jr. b. 10/1/1792 d. 11/24/1860 H554
Tyson	Patience I36 from Aisquith St.
Tyson	Isaac d. 1864 I36 unsure of date, from Aisquith St.
Tyson	Evan d. 1812 I37 from Aisquith St.
Tyson	Elizabeth d. 1826 I37 from Aisquith St.

U

Underhill	John C.	d. 8/21/1857	H500	age 52 y. 10 m. 11 d., of New York
unmarked	G51	from 10a book		
unmarked	G85			
unmarked	H294	in Webster plot		
unmarked	H320			
unmarked	H463	Baynes plot		
unmarked	I8			
unmarked	I57			
unmarked	I63			
unmarked	I64			
unmarked	I65			
unmarked	I233			
unmarked	I282			
unmarked	I491			
unmarked	H458	Baynes plot		
Updegraff	(Updegraph) Hannah E.	d. 6/29/1817	I132	age 61

van Trump	Rebecca H. Newbold	d. 9/4/1935	H399	age 96
van Trump	Mary Elizabeth	d. 3/30/1908	H400	age 76, daughter of Charles & Susan, H402/403, on map as von Trump
van Zile	Cornelius Richard	b. 3/25/1904	d. 2/25/1973	E32
van Zile	Merle R.	d. 10/31/1906	E32	
Vickers	E. W.	I249	no stone	
Vickers	W. N.	I250	no stone	

Vickers - Walton

Vickers   Rachel Dare   d. 7/18/1897   I256   age 69
Vickers   William M.   b. 5/27/1821   d. 3/18/1899   I257
Vickers   Martha M.   b. 9/12/1856   d. 3/4/1929   I258
Vickers   Edwin Thomas   d. 12/11/1933   I259   age 76
Von Valkenberg   Amelia   d. 1/11/1889   G72   age 62, no stone

W.   I.   d. 1816   616.
W.   D.   629
W.   W.   G86
Waddington   Marrianna E.   b. 8/10/1893   d. 4/3/1959   A133
Waddington   Henry Norman   b. 3/7/1887   d. 3/14/1941   A134
Waddington   Ernst Antone Sr.   b. 12/10/1851   d. 1/23/1936   A136
Waddington   Mary Ellen   b. 8/19/1853   d. 9/4/1906   A137
Walker   Mary Howard   d. 9/9/1932   B101   age 67, wife of Isaac, B102
Walker   Ava S.   d. 4/9/1941   B101 1/2   age 69 y. 4 m. 13 d.
Walker   Isaac H.   d. 4/13/1950   B102   age 84, husband of Mary, B101
Walker   Amelia Himes   b. 7/24/1880   d. 7/19/1974   E142   possibly E143
Walker   Robert Hunt   b. 10/23/1882   d. 7/1/1948   E143
Walker   Lucy Cooper   d. 5/28/1850   d. 5/8/1934   E144
Walker   Elisha Hunt   b. 8/4/1844   d. 4/24/1917   E145
Walker   James Talbott   d. 4/7/1885   E146   age 7 m. 20 d.
Walker   Elizabeth Cooper   d. 3/14/1895   E147   age 4 y. 1 m. 21 d.
Wallace   Amanda America   d. 7/19/1887   age 87, from 9b book
Walton   Robert H. Smith   b. 4/5/1913   d. 11/5/1937   A68
Walton   Dr. Henry Janney   b. 1/14/1879   d. 1/24/1965   A69
Walton   Helen Alford Smith   b. 4/14/1878   d. 1/22/1968   A70
Walton   Hannah   b. 1787   d. 1856   A90
Walton   Thornton   b. 1794   d. 1884   A90
Walton   Britton   A90   cremated

Walton Wilfred C. d. 4/7/1891 A91 age 3 y. 5 m., son of Ellen & William, A92/93, moved from E22 1921
Walton Clarence Wilfred d. 4/7/1891 A91 age 3
Walton Ellen S. b. 9/16/1845 d. 6/30/1928 A92 wife of William E., A93
Walton William E. b. 4/8/1851 d. 8/4/1947 A93 husband of Ellen S., A92
Waterhouse Ann b. 1763 d. 1841 I501
Watson Harry Selby b. 9/22/1896 d. 9/26/1969 A197 son of Harry Watson & Anna Gimmer
Watson Carola Read b. 11/22/1896 d. 11/10/1989 A198
Watson Martha Ann b. 1844 d. ?/?/? I322 age 12 m. 12 d.
Wayhill M. d. 1836 621
Weatherald William d. 9/26/1867 H470 age 60
Webb Mary d. 7/?/1851 H102 daughter of William B. & R.T.
Webster Elizabeth d. 2/20/1821 H216 age 74
Webster Sarah R. d. 1840 H259
Webster Daniel b. 1/22/1812 d. 9/?/1852 H260 unsure of dates
Webster Isaac H261 age 11 m.
Webster Priscilla d. 1/3/1854 H262 age 64
Webster Ida b. 6/1/1856 d. 9/9/1859 H263 unsure of death date
Webster Sophia H. d. 5/11/1862 H293 age 68
Webster children H295 of C. W. Webster
Webster Clara Whittingham b. 1861 d. 10/28/1934 H295 age 73 y. 1 m. 16 d.
Webster Charles Rigor b. 2/14/1857 d. 11/29/1905 H296
Webster Henry W. d. 7/12/1917 H321 age 47, no stone
Webster Sarah R. (C.) b. 12/30/1838 d. 9/3/1916 H322 daughter of Henry H. & Harriet J., H326/H327
Webster Grace b. 2/22/1854 d. 5/21/1942 H323 daughter of Henry H. & Harriet J., H326/H327
Webster Dr. Henry W. Jr. d. 8/29/1894 H324 age 64
Webster Rigor H324 from 3x5 card
Webster Catherine W. (E.) d. 2/20/1872 H325 age 42
Webster Caroline E. H325 from 1931 book, not on stone

Webster - Winslow

Webster Harriett J. b. 12/12/1811 d. 2/11/1900 H326 age 88 y. 2 m., wife of Henry W., H327

Webster Henry W. M.D. d. 10/23/1869 H327 age 72, husband of Harriett J., H326

Webster Charles W. d. 6/08/1907 H330 age 66, no stone

Weems Sutton Isaac d. 4/18/1900 I301 age 85

Weems Cassandra S. d. 1868 I303

Weigel Eleanor Eliza d. 1/3/1945 I182 age 88, buried with John Regester, unreadable stone

West William Street b. 11/12/1891 d. 11/26/1924 I361 son of William R West

West Sarah Ann McFarland b. 11/12/1867 d. 9/5/1935 I362

West William Ross b. 6/4/1857 d. 10/26/1935 I363

West Franklin Leavitt d. 9/3/1897 I366 age 16 m.

Whitaker Ann M. b 2/23/1800 d. 1/13/1871 H105

Whitaker N. P. b. 11/9/1830 d. 12/31/1850 H106

White Susan Harry b. 7/16/1919 d. 12/22/1947 A194 from 10a book A196

Whiteley S. A. d. 4/1/1812 601 unsure of date

Whitely Jane W. d. 5/3/1841 677

Wierman William d. 1873 I374 unsure of date, memorial stone

Wigham Mary Margaret b. 2/28/1891 d. 8/8/1908 G57

Williams William H. d. 1/8/1887 G26 age 35, no stone

Williams Laura V. b. 1883 d. 8/11/1958 I92

Willis Clara L. b. 12/31/1854 d. 3/24/1923 F77 lived in Hattie Troupe family 30 yrs.

Wilson David Sr. d. 1793 G77

Wilson David Jr. b. 1836 d. 1885 G77

Wilson Jane d. 1816 G78 age 60

Wilson Samuel d. 1835 G79 age 17

Wilson Ann d. 1851 I61

Winslow Lena Garry b. 1/29/1888 d. 9/18/1971 A106 wife of Caleb

Winslow Dorothy Massey b. 9/12/1891 d. 3/30/1975 A107 wife of George A108

Winslow - Wood

Winslow George Leiper b. 3/4/1893 d. 4/27/1982 A108 husband of Dorothy, son of Rebecca L. & Dr. Randolph, A118/119
Winslow Robert Garey b. 11/9/1920 d. 7/11/1944 A114 son of Caleb & Lena, A106
Winslow Randolph II b. 10/14/1906 d. 11/30/1945 A115 son of Edwards & Emma C.
Winslow Margaret Kable Massey b. 7/29/1876 d. 5/3/1967 A116 wife of Dr. Nathan, A117, on map as died 1957
Winslow Dr. Nathan b. 11/17/1878 d. 10/7/1937 A117 husband of Margaret, A116, son of Randolph & Rebecca, A118/A119
Winslow Rebecca Fay-ssoux Leiper b. 5/29/1856 d. 5/22/1941 A118 wife of Dr. Randolph, A119, daughter of John C. & Mary E. Leiper
Winslow Dr. Randolph b. 10/23/1892 d. 2/27/1937 A119, husband of Rebecca, A118, son of Dr. Caleb & Jane P., F54/F55
Winslow Richard A120 no stone
Winslow wife of Richard A121 no stone
Winslow Susan Russell b. 1/7/1828 d. 8/5/1910 E187 wife of Eliakim, E188
Winslow Saint Clair Spruill b. 4/18/1899 d. 8/18/1899 F52 son of Dr. Randolph & Rebecca, A118/A119
Winslow infants one d. 1909, one d. 1910 F52½ children of J. Leiper & Edwards F.
Winslow Julianna Randolph b. 5/15/1861 d. 8/13/1928 F53 daughter of Dr. Caleb & Jane P., F54/F55
Winslow Jane Perry b. 7/23/1839 d. 2/14/1910 F54 wife of Caleb, F55
Winslow Dr. Caleb b. 1/24/1824 d. 6/13/1895 F55 husband of Jane, F54
Winslow Dr. Nathan b. 1/4/1795 d. 8/29/1873 F56
Winslow Dr. John R. b. 11/8/1820 d. 2/13/1866 F57
Winslow Dr. John R. b. 6/10/1866 d. 6/25/1937 F70 husband of Elizabeth L. R., F71; son of Caleb & Jane, F54/F55
Winslow Elizabeth Lewis Reed b. 6/28/1869 d. 9/11/1936 F71 wife of Dr. John R., F70
Wirt Phillip I550 from 10a book
Wood William E. d. 3/11/1878 B2 age 49

Wood - Yardley

Wood Anna E. d. 7/24/1924 B59 age 79
Wood Lukens (Lukins) d. 1/22/1929 B60 age 86
Wood Mary L. Probst d. 7/31/1926 E14 daughter of William & Christina Wood
Wood Christina S. b. 6/11/1820 d. 12/27/1892 E15
Wood William b. 10/16/1818 d. 3/31/1901 E16
Woodward Mary E128 unreadable stone
Woolston Benjamin S. d. 1/18/1904 C118 age 79, husband of Rachel, C119
Woolston Rachel B. d. 11/13/1887 C119 age 62, wife of Benjamin S., C118
Worthington Grace J. d. 5/19/1865 H556 age 77, in Hopkins plot
Worthington Wilson d. 12/1/1852 I251 age 59
Worthington Elizabeth W. d. 3/20/1881 I252 age 71
Worthington H. Wilson d. 11/15/1879 I253 age 35
Worthington Louis B.W. d. 8/2/1850 I307
Wright Grace R. d. 5/31/1891 B25 age 82
Wright Eliza J. d. 1/30/1883 B26

Yardley Alice Turner d. 11/25/1951 H461/2 age 91, not on stone
Yardley Katherine d. 11/21/1891 H52 age 2 y. 3 m., daughter of William & Alice, H461/2, no stone

www.ingramcontent.com/pod-product-compliance
Lightning Source LLC
Chambersburg PA
CBHW071228160426
43196CB00012B/2452